The MicroKidz are here . . .

The time:	the very near future
The characters:	Thor Benson, a fifteen-year-old computer whizz-kid Kevin and Pamela Powell, his neighbours and friends.

They comprise the MicroKidz and, together with their high-tech computer know-how and Mr Chips, Thor's ingenious robot, they're heading for mystery and adventure.

Computer Mind Games is the second MicroKidz Mystery.

**Also by the same author,
and available in Knight Books:**

The Cagey Bee Byte

and coming soon . . .

Fission Chips
The C.A.S.E. of the Data Snatchers

THE MICROKIDZ MYSTERY ADVENTURES

THE MICROKIDZ MYSTERY ADVENTURES
THE MICROKIDZ MYSTERY ADVENTURES
THE MICROKIDZ MYSTERY ADVENTURES

THE MICROKIDZ MYSTERY ADVENTURES

Computer Mind Games

G. P. JORDAN

KNIGHT BOOKS
Hodder and Stoughton

THE MICROKIDZ MYSTERY ADVENTURES

First published in Canada by General Paperbacks 1984
First published in Great Britain by Knight Books 1984

British Library C.I.P.

Jordan, G. P.
Computer mind games.
I. Title
823′.914[J]   PZ7

ISBN 0 340 36530 7

The characters and situations in this book are entirely imaginary and bear no relation to any real person or actual happening

Printed and bound in Great Britain for Hodder and Stoughton Paperbacks, a division of Hodder and Stoughton Ltd, Mill Road, Dunton Green, Sevenoaks, Kent (Editorial Office: 47 Bedford Square, London, WC1 3DP) by Richard Clay (The Chaucer Press) Ltd, Bungay, Suffolk

Contents

CHAPTER 1
An Unexpected Guest

"Who's playing games with me now?" asked Edward Benson, as he entered the kitchen that morning.

His wife Laraine peered up from the table with a confused expression on her face.

"All I wanted was the *New York Times* CompuPrint," he continued. "But instead, there's a message saying 'CANCEL RESERVATIONS FOR CONVENTION'."

"If I didn't want you to go, dear, I'd ask in person," Mrs. Benson replied calmly. "Besides, I never use the computer this early in the morning."

Edward Benson reached for the glass of orange juice on the counter. Nearing middle age and greying slightly at the temples, he was a tall, sinewy man who still retained the physique he'd developed playing college basketball. Wearing a tailored, ivory shirt and navy tie with his light suit, he was preparing to leave for BenDaCon, his electronic data consultants office.

"Well, I won't be leaving for anywhere until I scan the news and TeleMail," he stated. "And who would want me to cancel out of that convention?"

Laraine Benson shrugged. Two years younger than her husband, Mrs. Benson had also aged elegantly. A daily exercise plan was as important to her as a proper night's sleep. The red and white track suit she wore was more for fitness than for fashion.

"Maybe Thor is trying to tell you something," she offered. "He's designing something special for the Science Fair."

"Any idea what he's up to?"

"He made me promise to keep it a secret," she replied. "He wants you to see the official demonstration."

Edward chuckled as he picked up a bran muffin. Whatever his son was experimenting with now would surely be interesting. Ever since Thor had been able to sit upright in a chair, he'd managed to maneuver himself in front of their microcomputer. At first, he'd played the joystick, winning consistently on the early game cartridges. That, however, soon bored him. Once the boy had discovered the purpose of the typewriter keyboard peripheral, a new world opened up. Thor had taught himself to read and write before entering elementary school.

"Has he given up breakfast lately?" Mr. Benson asked, as he checked the digital clock. "Maybe you should wake him up."

"He's not in his room. And I checked the lab."

Laraine was referring to the room behind the garage which Thor and her husband had converted into an electronics laboratory for building and testing new devices.

"I wonder what he's up to?" murmured the man. Then he returned to his earlier concern. "And what that message is about."

Bending over their home RND microcomputer, Edward typed in a request. He searched the input file register for the origin of the "CANCEL RESERVATIONS FOR CONVENTION" notice.

"It arrived twenty minutes ago," he reported, "but uncoded."

That did not satisfy him. An uncoded break-in onto their home micro was most unusual. This situation required his immediate attention.

Using the VistaPhone modem, Mr. Benson logged on to the mainframe computer at his office.

"That will track it down," he thought aloud.

Just then two shadows passed across the large kitchen window, and a moment later, Thor and his friend, Kevin Powell, came in through the side door. Between them they carried an oblong metal box.

"Hi, folks. Just coming back to make sure you weren't sleeping in," Thor said cheerfully. "And Kevin came for breakfast."

"Your second today?" Mr. Benson joked to the older boy from across the street.

"Let's call it an early lunch," smiled Kevin.

He and Thor set the metal container down on a side counter.

"Take it easy," warned Mrs. Benson. "There are enough scratches there already."

"I'm always careful, Mom. Especially when you're here."

At fifteen years of age, Thor often spoke boldly to his parents. As an only child, Thor had received his parents' full attention in his upbringing, becoming the image of his father in the process. In fact, Mrs. Benson sometimes called one by the other's name.

"Anything for me on the TeleMail?" asked Thor.

"I haven't been able to find out yet. Do you have any reason for not wanting me to attend the convention?"

Thor looked confused.

Mr. Benson explained that when he'd dialed up for the

morning CompuPrint news, a peculiar message had appeared instead.

"Honest, I haven't used the RND in two days," Thor replied. "I've been busy with Kevin."

"That's right, Mr. Benson. We've been using his portable micro in the lab. It's perfect for our experiments."

"Your mother thought you might have set that instruction in to get me to stay behind for the Science Fair," Edward told them, as he stood up. "What about a preview?"

"We still need a few days to tune it properly."

The man nodded, then bid the pair farewell as he left the room.

Mrs. Benson followed her husband to the front door, where he picked up a small suitcase. They left together, since Laraine was also driving into midtown Stanton.

Meanwhile, Kevin and Thor checked the RND microcomputer. Despite new commands, the video display monitor continued to read out the strange notice.

"There must be a branch leak," suggested Kevin.

Before offering his own guess, Thor conducted some rapid tests. This was what he loved most about computers: finding new patterns within billions of possibilities, leading to answers of questions never before asked.

Kevin knew when to stand aside and let his friend take control. Although he was taller and more muscular than his light-featured pal, Kevin felt secondary in scientific matters. Kevin had shades of brilliance too, though he often needed encouragement to act on his ideas. His mother, Kay Powell, was the mathematics teacher at Stanton High School, and was well liked by all the students. That Kevin and his sister Pamela would be good at math was hardly surprising. That living across the street from Thor Benson they would grow up together and share in his discoveries in the computer world was only natural. And lucky.

"Weird," muttered Thor at the keyboard. "Every instruction leads to a blank response. Or to the 'CANCEL' notice."

He paused to consider the situation. His dark blue eyes darted over the micro unit before settling on the RND Peripheral case underneath the printer. Within seconds he had it open, and the contents spread on the floor.

"Somehow, I feel that message is stored and reentering itself from here," he speculated.

"And if it isn't, you'll have a bigger mess to clear up."

Just as Thor was prying open the relay connectors, he heard a knock on the door. It startled him and he dropped the panel.

"Can you answer that, Kevin?"

Moments later, he saw Pamela Powell enter the room. She was a slight, dark-haired girl, whose shy smile and personality Thor secretly found attractive. Pam was a year younger than her brother and the same age as Thor. Fortunately for her, he often joked, the only thing she had in common with Kevin was her surname.

"Is this what happens when your parents leave the house?" asked Pamela, observing the scattered components. "You can't avoid tearing the place apart."

"Just doing some trouble-shooting."

Kevin explained the problem, while Thor continued his primary investigation. While he was finishing, Pamela sat down in the chair and pressed the input command.

Instantly, the computer came to life, with the Compu-Print news data popping onto the screen.

"How did you do it?" the astonished boys asked.

"Easy," Pam replied, with a wave of her index finger.

"All it needed was a woman's touch."

The two boys countered with mild laughter. While they were enjoying her joke, the computer shut down once more.

"That'll teach you," Pam told them.

"I'm going to get to the bottom of this if. . ." Thor began, then his words dropped off.

"If what?" probed Kevin.

"If it kills you."

Now Pamela had a laugh on her brother. She and Thor shared a keen sense of humor, perhaps to compensate for their shy personalities.

After trying for another ten minutes to get the RND micro functioning, Thor admitted defeat.

"I don't believe it," whistled Pam. "Our genius has been stumped."

"But only for a short time," he countered. "We'll put my portable unit onto this and take some readings."

He motioned for Kevin to accompany him out to the lab.

Pamela stayed in the control chair. She was hoping to try a test of her own, but stopped short when she heard her name whispered from the kitchen.

"Quiet! Come here!"

Thor's voice had a tone of nervousness.

Entering the hallway, she looked into the kitchen. She was puzzled to see her brother and Thor crouching at the window, peering cautiously outside.

"Get down Pam," Thor implored. "Or the man will see you!"

Now, Pamela glanced out the rear window toward the garage. There, standing in the doorway, about to enter Thor's laboratory, was a stranger, wearing a business suit and dark glasses.

Kevin indicated that the pair remain silent. He moved to the side door, hoping to catch the intruder unaware. Thor followed. Pamela peeked over the window ledge, as the boys crept through the backyard toward the lab. The man was turned away from them.

Just as Kevin lunged at the stranger, they heard a horrifying growl coming from inside the dark interior.

Suddenly, a black and tan Doberman pinscher, fangs damp and gleaming, sprang onto Kevin!

CHAPTER 2

Missing Matter

The powerful animal drove Kevin to the ground. The boy writhed, attempting to force his foot against the dog's throat. A piercing scream brought Pamela into the backyard. The stranger in dark glasses moved toward the struggle.

"Prince! Halt! Stand clear!" he shouted.

The Doberman froze. The stranger snapped his fingers twice, and the dog returned to its master. Thor and Pamela, having stood helplessly by until now, ran to Kevin and helped him up.

"Please excuse his conduct," said the man, while patting the dog's head. "Prince has been highly trained for defense, as well as guidance."

"You've no business sneaking onto other people's property!" Kevin shouted in a frightened voice.

"That dog is vicious!" Pamela added angrily. "It should be locked up!"

Once he was certain that Kevin wasn't hurt, Thor gave close scrutiny to this unexpected visitor. The man appeared to be in his fifties, and wore a dark suit which seemed inappropriate for such a fine day. He spoke with a mild European accent. The dark glasses, however, provided the clue to a most surprising discovery.

"You said the dog is trained for guidance?" asked Thor.

The stranger took a short step. His foot caught the floor beam, and he nearly collapsed. Thor impulsively moved to catch the man. The Doberman growled, and the boy froze. Somehow, the intruder caught hold of the doorframe and remained standing.

What Thor had suspected now became obvious to the Powells. The stranger was blind!

"That is correct," he told them. "Prince is a special Seeing Eye dog. He assists me in getting around, and if I am otherwise threatened, he reverts to the more basic canine instinct."

"Very effectively," admitted Thor. "But why were you trespassing?"

"From that assured tone of voice, I must be talking to Thor Benson."

Pamela and Kevin, still shaking from their altercation, looked over at their friend. They waited as Thor studied the man closely, reluctant to speak.

"Who are you, and why were you prowling around here?" demanded the boy.

The stranger shuffled forward, with the Doberman obediently moving alongside. As if directed by a sixth sense, the man made his way up to Thor and extended his hand.

"I'm Willard Stong, and I've waited some time to meet you."

"That's all very nice, Mr. Stong, but it doesn't explain why you're here with a dog that nearly injured my friend."

"For that I apologize. And do call me Willard. But as

you are about to hear, there are important reasons why I came unannounced. Is there a place we can sit and talk?"

Thor led Willard Stong to the shaded patio lounge in the back garden. Prince paced silently nearby, sitting at the man's feet as he was helped to a chair. Kevin remained wary of the animal and took a place by Pamela on the log bench. They waited for Willard to speak.

The story unraveled over the course of an hour. The youngsters sat spellbound, as Stong recounted a series of mysterious messages he had intercepted at a government TeleData agency. All the material related to scientific research being conducted by a firm located here in Stanton. Thor recognized the name of the company—Megadapt Research—but knew nothing of its operation. It had only opened within the last month. He did recall, however, that Megadapt had made a peculiar announcement about none of its research having a military application.

"Well, I happen to know that is untrue."

The group remained silent for some moments. Thor came to the most obvious conclusion.

"Megadapt must have an ultraconfidential contract to fulfill and, for security reasons, are claiming otherwise," the boy surmised. "It's not unlikely, since there are over a hundred high-tech companies around Stanton. If the government decides something needs to be kept secret, that's their privilege. It's the price we pay for security."

"But what if that work is not being done for *our* government," Willard Stong countered.

Kevin and Pamela listened earnestly to the conversation. Having shared many adventures with their neighbor, they were accustomed to unusual encounters. And they had learned that patience was a valuable asset in matters both scientific and investigative. As Thor often reminded them, the processes were similar. One had to dedicate a certain amount of time to an experiment—or investigation—before the truth unfolded.

The blind man reached to his side and patted the Doberman. Apparently it calmed his nerves, for when he began again, he spoke quietly. He told the trio he'd heard Thor being interviewed on the "Computer Focus" satellite program a few weeks previously. The show told the story of *THE CAGEY BEE BYTE* mystery at a summer computer camp. A scientist had disappeared after completing research in the use of microcircuits and honeybees for crop pollination. A criminal element infiltrated the locality on behalf of a foreign enemy power. With the aid of Pamela and Kevin Powell, Thor had alerted the military to the dangerous situation.

This had been the latest in a series of adventures involving Thor and the Powells, whom the press had nicknamed "The MicroKidz," because of their ingenuity with microsystems.

"So, I have come to you out of frustration," concluded the man, as he rose to his feet. "Consider what I have said to be completely confidential. I will contact you tomorrow."

The blind man asked Thor to call a taxi. He declined Kevin's offer to be driven home, insisting on his independence. The three youths accompanied the man and his obedient guide dog to the sidewalk, and waited for the cab.

Again, Willard Stong implored their confidentiality. A Stanton Checkered cab arrived shortly after, and the stranger and his dog were whisked away.

"What do you make of that?" breathed Pamela.

The boys remained silent, watching the cab move off down the tree-lined street. The trio kept their thoughts to themselves as they walked slowly back across the front lawn. Willard Stong's reason for seeking out Thor Benson would soon be disclosed. But, for Kevin Powell, there was a more immediate concern.

"Hey, my stomach is rumbling," he declared.

"I thought that sound was a thunderstorm approaching," his sister interjected.

"There will be if I don't eat soon!"

A familiar brown station wagon pulled into the driveway across the street. The trio changed direction to hurry over to greet Mrs. Powell.

"You're just in time, Mom!"

Kay Powell looked at her grinning son and laughed.

"Let me guess," she said, hitting him playfully in the stomach. "The internal hunger alarm is ringing."

"Loud and clear," reported Kevin.

"Maybe you should work some of your breakfast off first," Mrs. Powell remarked. She moved to the sliding rear door of the car and pointed to the parcels inside. "Start with these Kevin. After all, Pam and I won't get to see much more of these groceries."

Inside the Powell house, while Pamela and her mother went into the kitchen to unpack and talk, Thor followed Kevin to his bedroom. The older boy had soundproofed the walls to confine the noise of his quadrophonic music system. Performers being heard on the laserdisc video player also appeared on the four old television sets Kevin had installed. It always amazed Thor that, with all this going on, Kevin still expected him to take part in a conversation.

While Kay Powell prepared a meal in the microwave, she asked her daughter if she'd heard of any problems lately between Mr. and Mrs. Benson. The two families had lived opposite each other for years and shared many experiences. They'd become particularly close after Mr. Powell abandoned his wife and two youngsters. The Bensons had been very supportive during the painful months surrounding the Powell's divorce, helping Kay to overcome her bitterness and reestablish herself as a highly regarded math instructor.

"No, Mom, you know how the Bensons are. Not a care in the world, happy as can be."

"I know they've always seemed that way, dear," confided the woman. "But the oddest thing occurred earlier. As I drove out of the supermarket, they passed by in their car. Now you know I'm not a road racer . . ."

"—like Kevin," interjected the girl.

"Right, but since we were headed in the same direction, I sped up to pull alongside them," she continued. "Now I realize some people consider it rude to honk and wave while driving, but they are our neighbors. Well, for some reason they didn't bother to wave back. Maybe they were having a serious discussion with the man in the rear, I don't know."

"Thor said his Dad has been working around the clock," Pamela offered as an excuse. "I wouldn't worry about it. Let's get lunch ready—or Kevin won't be talking to us."

"Is that all it takes?" laughed Mrs. Powell.

During the meal, Mrs. Powell was too busy fielding inquiries from Thor regarding Theories of Probability to mention the peculiar incident on the road. It had become a recurring theme each time the boy ate here. Mrs. Powell and Pam shared a joke: the probability that Thor would not somehow get around to discussing a Theory of Probability was directly proportional to the seriousness of his current adventure.

Thor thanked Mrs. Powell, as he excused himself from

the table. The woman wondered if his thanks were for the food or the information. She suspected the latter.

Crossing the street, Thor Benson wondered when he would hear from Willard Stong again. The blind man had seemed sincere, but Thor remained puzzled by his story.

Back in his own living room, Thor was confronted by the mass of peripheral components, spread out on the floor as he'd left them. Glancing at the display monitor atop the RND computer, his attention was caught by a multicolored graphics pattern scanning itself at random. The "CANCEL RESERVATIONS FOR CONVENTION" notice was no longer flashing on the screen.

Thor studied the output for a moment. He attached a Tracer diskette to the RND and recorded the data.

A short time later, Kevin Powell came to the house. Anxious to resume experiments on their secret entry to the Science Fair, he left Thor alone to work on the RND and went to the kitchen to retrieve the oblong metallic box.

"Okay," he sighed, returning quickly from the kitchen. "Where did you hide it?"

"Hide what?" Thor asked.

"Our Nobel prizewinner."

Suddenly Thor bolted to his feet. One look at his face told Kevin what had happened.

The oblong metallic box was gone.

Each turned to the other and, having come to the same conclusion simultaneously, blurted out together, "Willard Stong!"

CHAPTER 3
Into the Den of Intrigue

Thor moved swiftly to the compucorner in the hallway. There he punched the VistaPhone program button for the Stanton Checkered Taxi Company. Within seconds, the picture of an old dispatcher appeared on the screen.

"Stanton Checkered," said the man, who then noted the two-way location identifier at the bottom of the screen. "You are at 208 Matrix Boulevard, and where will you be going?"

"I need to know where the man you picked up here an hour ago was dropped off," said the boy quickly.

They watched as the dispatcher entered the request onto his terminal. By his slow movements, the man seemed to be either very tired or very bored with his job.

"Passenger and guide dog conveyed to Megadapt Research Facility, which is . . ."

"Okay!" interrupted Thor. "I know just where that is. Thank you."

"Anytime, pal," replied the dispatcher, as the VistaPhone screen went blank.

So Willard Stong had gone to the very place where he'd reported strange things in progress! And the metal box holding their Science Fair project had disappeared shortly after he left them. It seemed that Stong now had two matters to explain.

Thor decided he'd better implement some defenses before setting off on Stong's trail. Kevin hurried into the backyard laboratory after his friend.

In the spacious room that was formerly the Benson's garage, Thor took a mental note of all the equipment present. He went to the electronics bench at the rear, where a laser-cutting lathe held a circular microchip assembly case. A touch switch activated the device. Kevin stood back, shielding his eyes from the white-hot flame.

"We're not leaving here until I finish adjusting Mr. Chips," Thor stated. "Can't afford to have any other strangers taking whatever they want."

"There's too many parts and tools to leave unguarded," Kevin agreed. "And none of them have patents."

"Yet," his friend added.

A small domestic robot rested on the workbench by the laser lathe. Affectionately called "Mr. Chips," it was constructed from surplus parts and test hardware. Though a microchip memory powered its activity, at times the unit almost demonstrated real feelings. To the Benson family, Mr. Chips had all the lovable qualities of a household pet. And home security was his specialty.

Once the assembly case was pierced, and a cluster of photodetectors added to its base, Thor motioned for Kevin to assist. The metal oxide semiconductor transmitters would indicate the change in light presence. They would pick up natural infrared body heat from a human intruder entering a specific area, and then register an alarm.

"Hold this steady," requested the boy. "I'm going to put in a new remote scanner."

Carefully, Thor rotated the laser lathe. Perfect indentations were made beneath the photodetector cluster. The piece was soon installed, and the robot began operating.

"Okay, Chips, stand on guard for thee," Kevin chuckled.

They placed the robot in the house and put on the delay activator. Thor stepped over the mass of peripherals still on the floor, reminding himself to tidy the place on his return.

"What do you make of that?" Kevin wondered, looking again at the odd graphics pattern passing through the RND video display monitor every few seconds.

"I don't know just yet," Thor stated, "But I have a feeling it's coming from the same source that sent the message to Dad this morning."

He picked up the bag of observation gear he kept stored near the RND, and they left the house by the back door. All the entrances were sealed by the electromagnetic field now emanating from Mr. Chips.

Kevin backed his sports car onto the road, as Thor double-checked his seat belt. He did so with good reason, since Kevin's reputation for fast driving was quickly reaffirmed. The trees and houses on Matrix Boulevard soon became a continuous blur, as the vehicle shot down the street and onto the expressway ramp.

Thor always enjoyed the ride along the elevated motorway. From above, one could see the modern town of Stanton, with its gleaming glass and steel towers, nestled into the green pasture lands of the surrounding farms.

Until ten years ago, Stanton had been a typical country village, with a single general store, a post office, and a dozen houses nearby. Then the microelectronics boom had hit, and high-tech companies like Megadapt were desperate for more laboratory and warehouse space. Existing urban centres were already overcrowded, so the only alternative was to move out to the country and build new cities there. Some small farmers had to be bought out, but those that remained benefited from the new technology. Their farms now produced far more than they'd ever dreamed possible.

Thor Benson often thought how lucky he was to live in Stanton. He was fascinated by anything to do with electronics and space research, but he also felt the need, sometimes, to escape to the clean-smelling fields surrounding his town. It was good knowing he had the choice of where to spend his free time: in the exciting environment of high-tech industry, or in the peaceful slow-moving setting of a farmer's field. Computers and cows both held an attraction for him.

"We're gettng close," said Kevin.

He pointed to the Megadapt Research sign, posted above the expressway exit ramp and brought the car to a halt in the emergency lane. This vantage point permitted the youths to look down onto the grounds of the company. A ten-foot high fence, no doubt carrying an electrical charge, bordered the perimeter of the lot. Two buildings occupied the central area, with a parking lot between them. A guardhouse secured the entrance and exit.

"Looks like all the others," Kevin muttered.

"They all do from a distance," added Thor. "The only way to find out is to go inside."

This brought a nervous laugh from Kevin.

"Right. You expect to walk up, tell your name to the guard, and be let in?"

Thor continued to observe the area.

"That's exactly what I'm going to do."

"What makes you think they'll let you in?" wondered Kevin. "I mean, the place has a five-star security rating. It's off-limits."

Raising his arm, Thor pointed to a door opening at the rear of a building. They could not see the face of the person in the shadows, but they could clearly see the Doberman pinscher that came out after him.

"Count me out," shuddered Kevin. "One a day is my absolute limit for those killer canines."

"Hey, it's just part of the Megadapt patrol."

They watched as the dog paced by the side of the building. The youths were about to get back into the sports car, when they saw the rear door of the building open again. This time a man came all the way out.

"Hand me the travel bag," said Thor.

He took out his high-powered OptoScope and adjusted it. Raising the unit to his eyes, he zoomed in on the man and dog.

"Gotcha!" he chuckled.

The man patting the Doberman was wearing dark glasses. By pressing on the top button, Thor could record the image on a minidisk. That done, he passed the OptoScope over to Kevin.

"Willard Stong!" Kevin said.

"And all recorded for posterity," Thor added, with a tap to the unit. "Or for evidence."

The two youths climbed back into the car and drove on down the ramp. While Kevin attended to driving safely across two lanes of moving traffic, Thor took a tiny metal clip from his bag. He slipped off his track shoes to insert it.

"Listen, Thor. About that dog. I really don't want to go near the place."

"You're not going to, Kev. Just let me off at the corner. I'll go in on my own."

"Just like that, huh?" Kevin shook his head. "I don't believe it."

"Just watch me," came Thor's reply to the challenge. "Drive back up the ramp. And don't worry, I've got my tracker on." He patted the shoe which concealed the metal clip.

After letting Thor out at the nearest stoplight, Kevin made a U-turn and headed back to the same spot to watch.

Once alone, Thor took a deep breath before walking the three hundred yards to the security guardhouse. He watched a company van on the other side get clearance to leave before the gate swung open. Kevin had been correct in saying this was a five-star security operation; nothing came or went without undergoing close scrutiny.

"What do you want here?" a young guard asked gruffly.

"I'm here to see Mr. Willard Stong," replied the boy, in a calm manner.

"What's your name?" the guard asked, without batting an eye.

He told Thor to wait while he relayed the information on the intercom inside the booth. Thor, meanwhile, took note of the surveillance cameras peering down from the buildings and guardhouse. Along the bottom portion of the surrounding wire fence, he saw the bodies of several dead rabbits.

"Certainly does have a strong charge," he thought, looking at the electrified fence.

The guard came out with a small blue laminated card.

"You'll have to stick this on your shirt, kid," the man told him. "Or you might get hurt." The guard laughed at his own joke. Thor did not. "Now go over to the A block and go in door E-3."

With the ID card pinned to his shirt, Thor walked through the revolving pedestrian gate and into the grounds of the facility. Over on the expressway ramp, he saw Kevin watching. His friend waved, but Thor did not return the gesture. He wanted to avoid arousing any suspicion.

Door E-3 was the same one that Willard Stong and his dog had used a short time before. Just as he knocked, E-3 swung open to Thor.

"Come this way, Mr. Benson," said another security guard, in a flat tone.

The first thing Thor noticed inside the building was a high-pitched tone sounding incessantly. Thor raised his hands to his ears to block it out.

"You'll get used to it," shouted the guard over the noise.

It was then that Thor noticed that the man wore miniature earplugs. A shudder of anticipation went through his body. Everything seemed poised for action. As they walked down the darkened corridor, the ringing tone decreased.

Suddenly, loud barking shattered the uneasy atmosphere. A black and tan Doberman pinscher bolted across the corridor.

The security guard stopped and indicated that Thor was to step into a side room. A shaft of sunlight came through an elongated window, the only touch of warmth in the room. The area resembled the waiting lounge in an old dentist's office. Its sole purpose was to calm anxious visitors by giving them nothing to concentrate on. Thor took a seat in one of the three large chairs. He could still hear the high-pitched sounds increasing and decreasing in volume, broken only by occasional barking from the guard dogs. Thor believed there was some kind of ultrasonic detector set up around the interior perimeter of the building.

After twenty minutes of waiting, he decided to check the corridor and call the guard. To his surprise, the door was locked. Thoughts of dread began to flash through his mind, as the bolt turned suddenly, without warning.

"Will you follow me please?" asked a tall muscular man in a three-piece suit.

The security guard who had brought Thor to his office was also waiting to escort the boy. The muscles in Thor's stomach clenched into a tight knot. As he walked down the corridor between these two silent adults, the youngster could think only of how much he missed his parents.

Finally, they came to an open atrium. The tall man in the suit motioned for Thor to take a seat by the window. The security guard took up a position by the entrance.

"I'm sorry for the delay, but we have been conducting an interrogation, Thor. My name is Samuel Norse and I'm the director of security."

"I'd like to speak with Mr. Stong."

"Right now you are speaking with me," said the man sternly. "And I am interested in why you have come here without any advance notice."

"Mr. Stong can probably answer that for you," Thor said, in his determined way.

"I'd prefer you to."

Thor saw the security guard watching him with a mocking smile on his face. He was clearly outnumbered and at their command.

"He paid a visit to my house today. And he didn't give any advance notice either. After Mr. Stong left, I discovered that a device I was working on was missing."

"And you believe he knows of its whereabouts?"

The boy nodded.

"Excuse my curiosity, but why would such a renowned scientist be interested in some schoolboy's machine?"

Thor slowly began to redden with irritation.

"That's what I want to know."

Seeing that the youngster was becoming upset, Samuel Norse tried to soothe him with conversation.

"Tell me what this device of yours is for," he smiled. "You know, we at Megadapt are very interested in what young minds are thinking."

Thor didn't feel this was the best time for such a discussion and told the man so. He also reiterated his request to see Willard Stong. If that could not be arranged, then he would leave the premises and come another time.

"I'm afraid it won't be possible for you to leave right now," Samuel Norse replied. "You may have to wait until Mr. Stong returns to the facility."

"But I just saw him outside this building."

"A while ago, perhaps. In the meantime, you can enjoy the comforts of our waiting area."

Norse gave a brusque nod and left. The security guard motioned for Thor to follow him back down the hall.

Glancing through the atrium window into the parking lot, Thor recognized the familiar form of Willard Stong.

In a puzzling turn of events, he saw the blind man climb into the driver's seat of a light green vehicle.

It was the Benson family car!

CHAPTER 4

Beyond Control Sequences

Kevin Powell had developed a cramp in his arms from holding the OptoScope in a fixed position for so long. He was also bored at the inactivity in the yard of the complex. From his vantage point in the emergency lane of the expressway ramp, Kevin saw nothing to indicate what his friend was undergoing. He was accustomed to Thor investigating tricky situations, often disappearing for long periods of time, but he always reappeared safely.

When half an hour had elapsed, with still no sign of Thor, Kevin decided to check for messages back at the house. He reached into the car for the cellular radiophone. Dialing an open frequency, Kevin punched in the Powell home code number. Within moments, the sound of Pamela's voice came through the car speaker.

"Why didn't you respond to my Alert call?"

"I haven't been in the car for awhile. What's up?"

"There's something strange going on over at the Benson house," came the reply. "A van is parked in their driveway. Whoever is inside is just sitting and waiting."

Kevin bit his lip. "What sort of van is it?"

"A white one."

"I mean, does it have an identifying sign?"

In the resulting silence, Kevin visualized Pam going to the window to check.

"No, not a thing," she replied. "Hold on, and I'll run the license number into the county vehicle databank."

"Why didn't you do that before?"

His sister did not respond. Still gripping the Opto-Scope, Kevin sat up on the back of the sports car to continue his surveillance of the area. He focused the lens on a man walking in the parking lot, and watched as Willard Stong climbed into the driver's seat of a familiar green vehicle.

"Kevin, are you listening?"

"Go ahead," he told her, continuing to track Willard.

"The van at the Bensons' is registered to the Megadapt Research Facility," came the answer.

"Just as I thought. Okay, Pamela, now I want to run these numbers through the databank," he said, and started reading out the license plate on the green car.

"Hey, is this a joke or something?" Pam asked, after a short pause.

"Can't you find it?"

"That's the Bensons' car," declared Pamela. "Where are you anyway?"

"Looking down on the Megadapt property," he said, trying to answer calmly. "And right now, I'm watching our friend Willard Stong drive away in Mr. Benson's car."

"What? But he's blind!"

"And driving very well for someone in that condition."

The vehicle approached the guardhouse at the entrance, clearing through the security without even stopping.

Kevin had to make a choice: should he stay and watch

over the building where his friend remained, or should he pursue the mysterious man?

"What are you going to do?" crackled Pam's voice over the cellular radiophone.

"You notify Sergeant Dalby," Kevin told her, referring to a friend in the Stanton Police Department. "Have him check out those people in the Bensons' driveway. I'm going to follow Mr. Stong."

As he finished speaking, Kevin already had his sports car speeding down the expressway ramp. He planned to cut in behind Stong. The man was still wearing his dark glasses, yet here he was, with no Seeing Eye dog, driving at full speed along the expressway going into Stanton!

"Sergeant Dalby is on his way, Kevin," reported Pamela. "I also told him about the Bensons' car being stolen, and all police units have been notified."

"Thanks, sis. I'm trailing Stong on the Cartesian Freeway, just passing the sign for Van Allen Field."

Kevin hoped she would relay this reference point to the Stanton Police force. Usually, their cruisers patrolled this stretch of highway, since it passed over the central business district. For some odd reason, Kevin didn't sight any today. A stroke of bad luck, he thought.

The further they drove, the more Kevin began to wonder what the real purpose was to Willard Stong's surprise visit. Why had the man claimed to be blind? Was the whole Benson family entrapped at Megadapt? Where was Stong going in the Bensons' car? Every question raised more doubts and fears in Kevin's mind.

As if replaying the drive out to the Megadapt location, Kevin found himself going back along the same streets. The stranger was returning to the Bensons'!

Police cars, with patrolmen standing nearby, were parked in front of the house on Matrix Boulevard. It was the happiest, most reassuring sight Kevin could imagine. And, driving right into the trap, was Willard Stong. A few curious neighbors stood on front lawns to watch the scene. As his sports car screeched to a halt in their driveway, Pamela Powell came running out of the house.

"Don't do a thing!" she told him.

"What do you mean?"

"They say that everything is under control," she blurted. "Dalby and his men have been talking to the people in the van. Then he came over and told me not to worry, or to make any other calls."

"What's it all about?"

"You see that man?" Pamela pointed to a figure moving inside the Bensons' living room. "He went in there about ten minutes ago. Carried in a load of microtesters."

Kevin watched the action taking place around him, confused by the sequence of events. Certainly, things were *not* in control, he thought. The Bensons were nowhere in the vicinity, and strangers were entering their house under police guard.

"Tell me, how'd Stong do it?" Pam asked, referring to the amazing driving accomplishment of the blind man.

Her question focused Kevin's attention back to the man he'd been following. Stong had parked the Bensons' car alongside the van in their driveway. One of the men had gotten out of the van and had begun conversing with Stong as if they were old acquaintances. Stong then called for Sergeant Dalby, and the policeman hurried to his side.

"Can you believe what we're seeing?" Kevin whistled in amazement. "One minute we think he's a thief, and the next minute he has the police running at the snap of a finger."

"I still don't know what's going on," admitted Pamela.

"Mom told me earlier how Mr. and Mrs. Benson ignored her in the shopping plaza. She said there was a man sitting in the back seat of their car and . . ."

"A kidnapper!" Kevin exclaimed.

"That's just what I reported to Sergeant Dalby when you said their car was stolen," she said. "But he didn't seem to care for any other details."

"Well, I'm going to find out why!"

The youth jogged down his driveway and over to his neighbor's house. A policeman standing at the curb raised his arm.

"Stay right there, kid. This property is under guard."

"Yeah, that's pretty obvious," Kevin replied with a laugh. "I'd like to have a word with Sergeant Dalby. He knows who I am."

"Oh, yeah?" scoffed the officer.

"Seriously, we've worked together," Kevin continued, to the policeman's growing derision.

"Right, sonny. Just stay put."

Kevin was very angry. He had tried to convey important information to the superior officer on the scene and had been thwarted. The parents of his best friend were missing, and here was this grinning constable ordering him away. The boy stepped back to put the policeman off guard.

"Hey, Dalby!" shouted Kevin. Several officers turned to look at the youth. The Sergeant peered up from among a group standing by the van. "Yes, you! Come here!"

The command took everyone by surprise, but this rude outburst had the exact result Kevin intended. The policeman left the group and came down the driveway to meet the anxious boy.

"You have to listen to me, sir," Kevin said in distress. "Something very strange is going on!"

He told Dalby about Willard Stong's blindman act, the missing Science Fair experiment, and Thor going to Megadapt on the trail of Stong. Finally, he mentioned the Bensons' kidnapping.

"You've got a wild imagination," Sergeant Dalby smiled.

"But it's true. They just disappeared!"

"Cool your circuits, Kevin, everything is okay."

"Oh, yeah? So what are you going to do?"

"Ask you to step aside," said the Sergeant, looking over the boy's shoulder. "And let the family park here."

Kevin spun around. Coasting to a stop in a Stanton Checkered taxi were Mr. and Mrs. Benson, and Thor!

CHAPTER 5

The Memory Fill

"It's a violation of our rights!"

Edward Benson jabbed his finger at Willard Stong. The two men were standing in the living room, surrounded by the Powells, Thor, and his mother.

"If you wanted to examine my son's work, all that was necessary was a simple request."

"We could not afford any mistakes," Stong replied. "We needed an independent probe. And the test results prove us correct in our actions."

At stake was the seizure of the Science Fair exhibit which Kevin and Thor had constructed. Though the boys had initially built it for one reason, unknown to them, it had a far greater application.

"As a transceiver, Tempest-T is a potent device," continued Stong. "It has the capacity to both send and receive electron emissions that have escaped from computers many miles away."

He turned to the boys sitting on the couch.

"I'm certain they had no idea what the strategic applications of such an invention might be," concluded Stong.

Edward defended the youth's work by saying that their

intention was certainly not to develop military hardware, but to excel in a school project.

"That's all very well, Mr. Benson. But the fact remains that the Tempest-T device does have the potential to breach our security," countered the man. "And since Megadapt Research has a military contract, we felt that anyone able to trace the data flowing through our computers needed investigation."

"What's your contract for?" asked Thor, anxious to get the whole story.

"Of course, that is confidential, but I can assure you it is of vital importance. Now, to return to the matter of this machine of yours," Stong continued, pointing to Thor. "If it can trace and translate computer storm emissions, you may have a valuable invention."

Everyone understood that if the design were a success, patents, license agreements, and manufacturing offers would follow. It meant a possible fortune for the inventors.

"By the way," interjected Kevin. "When you were here before, you gave us another story about Megadapt. Like they weren't really working for our benefit and had secret foreign connections. What's the truth?"

"It's all true," Stong told them, "though part of my story may have been exaggerated. You see, it was my job to keep you three youngsters in the backyard while my associates, shall we say, 'removed' that metal box containing the Tempest-T."

Laraine Benson had stayed in the background until now, but she was also disturbed by the intrusion into her home. She demanded to know why she and her husband had been brought to the Megadapt building if the machine had already been removed.

"Again, another precaution on our behalf," explained

the man. "I'm very sorry that we upset part of your day, but you must realize that when the government grants a classified military contract, and some of our information is found to be leaking into an outside computer bank, we are forced to take unusual measures."

"Even when those measures infringe upon our basic rights?" Mr. Benson asked warily.

Willard Stong nodded, acknowledging that sometimes the law had to be bent to accommodate state security. He seemed to feel that this ended the discussion, but Pamela raised another unanswered question.

"How is it, Mr. Stong, that you are blind and can drive?"

"Clinically speaking, yes, I am completely blind. However, as you all know, amazing discoveries have been made lately in the biotechnics field."

So that was his secret. Willard Stong had a micro-optic implant! The youngsters recalled the discussion earlier that day when his scientific credentials had been related. How easy it would be for such a brilliant mind to seek out an opportunity for restoring sight.

He shifted the dark glasses on his face to let them all see the composition of the frame. It appeared to be made up of strands of fibre-optics.

"It's the CompuBlindsight system," he explained.

A knock on the door turned their attention to a new visitor. Megadapt's security director, Samuel Norse, entered, carrying the oblong metal container.

"We've checked the unit thoroughly," he explained to the Bensons and Mrs. Powell. "As you are aware, your boys have stumbled onto something quite important."

Edward remained unimpressed with the man's comments.

"You've returned the Tempest-T in its original condition?" he asked, suspecting the obvious.

"I'm sorry, but a few components had to be extracted. For security purposes," Norse added. "At some point soon, they will be returned."

"Thank you very much for your interest in my son," he told them in a sharp voice. "I think you have explained your side, and now I would like it very much if you would leave so we can resume our normal lives."

Stong and Norse recognized the bitterness in the man's voice and departed. The families were finally alone together.

Kay Powell had found the whole experience terribly unnerving. She asked Edward if he could confirm the military contracts Megadapt was claiming to have.

"I'll try, but that still wouldn't alter the main issue here: that they simply came in and took over."

Edward and the three youngsters left his wife and Mrs. Powell alone in the front room. Out in the back laboratory, they found that the Tempest-T had indeed been returned. More importantly, however, they found Mr. Chips lying under the lamp on the floor.

"They deactivated his circuits," Thor explained.

"I guess when those men first got here, they found him going wild. His burglar detection panel was pulled off."

"Can you fix it?"

"Yeah, but it will take awhile."

"Now you see what happens when you fool around with science?" chided the man.

The youngsters nervously agreed. The day had some unexpected turns all right, and now they had to deal with the consequences.

"Open that thing up, will you?" Mr. Benson asked.

Thor took his invention out of its metal box. The

Tempest-T resembled a compact remote processing device. Mr. Benson looked at the intricate board, the crossed peripheral enclosure and its microassembly pattern. He nodded, impressed.

"And that's what's causing so much trouble," he chuckled.

"Not until they return some parts," Thor clarified. "I guess Megadapt wants to find out how it ticks."

"Well, I know one thing it does," his father pointed out. "It fed the 'CANCEL RESERVATIONS' notice into the RND micro."

"You're kidding. How?"

"Two weeks ago, I entered an acceptance to attend, using my office mainframe. But only if an assignment was completed. Had that not occurred, a back-up message canceling the reservations was to be transmitted," Edward said, as he tapped the Tempest-T. "Something unlocked the release of that cancelation notice. This has to be it."

He left the trio to work on repairing Mr. Chips. It seemed that the little robot meant more to them than the troublesome new invention.

"Just like kids," he thought to himself. "They've already forgotten how afraid we all were."

Back in the house, Mr. Benson sat down in front of his RND to resolve the question of Megadapt's claims. Using the RND modem, Edward logged on to his office mainframe computer and began typing data file requests. Because of the official use of his own private password code, Edward could access the resources of a confidential memory bank.

"MEGADAPT RESEARCH FACILITY, FOUNDED BY JOHN DUNN," he read from the central data compiler. "MR. DUNN IS PRESENTLY ON A ONE YEAR SABBATICAL, SAIL-

ING AROUND THE WORLD ON HIS YACHT. BEGINNING WITH THE CONSTRUCTION OF A TELECOMMUNICATIONS PRINTER EIGHT YEARS AGO, MR. DUNN EXPANDED HIS COMPANY'S GROWTH INTO THE EXPERIMENTAL TECHNOLOGY SECTOR."

The report continued with the listings of profits, shares traded, and patents granted. Mr. Benson scanned these and then, using a special request feature, he searched for the CURRENT CONTRACTS file. Three codes were absent, with "CLASSIFIED" listed in their place.

"They are on the military payroll," he told his wife later. "According to the RND search, the classified codes originated with the military."

"And that's all you can find out?" Laraine asked.

"It's all we need to know, dear. Megadapt seems to be exercising their rights and privileges," he admitted. "I just had to check on them for my own sake. If they didn't have those contracts, I would be calling for action. And fast."

Inside the lab, Mr. Chips began moving slowly across the floor. Just as the robot reached the edge of the room, it spun around and tumbled down. Pamela laughed.

"It's not funny!" Thor declared, in a peeved tone.

"But Chips is acting like a comedian," she said.

"That's because his memory circuits have been scrambled," Kevin told her. "You'd act the same way if somebody wiped your mind, too."

"You mean brainwashing?"

"I don't think we could brainwash you, Pam," Thor told her. "There isn't enough to work with."

The sly comment angered the girl. She punched Thor on the shoulder, then left the lab.

"I guess you insulted her," Kevin said.

"Sorry about that, but she shouldn't have been bugging me about Mr. Chips," the boy sighed. "I think of him like one of the family, sort of."

"You want to leave it until tomorrow?"

They decided to continue the robot repairs for a short while longer. While they worked, they discussed the Tempest-T.

"If I had known it was capable of transmitting as well as receiving, I would have changed things around," confessed Thor. "We were right about the computer storm radiations, though."

"Yeah, but what a way to have our Science Fair project get recognized," Kevin chuckled. "And we didn't even finish it!"

They laughed together at that.

Thor thought of how discoveries sometimes result in extraordinary applications not intended, or even visualized, by their originators. The classic example was Einstein's equation $E = mc^2$, which, through the interpretation of other minds, became the atomic bomb.

"Let's take a break," suggested Thor.

"Perfect timing. Satellite News is on soon," Kevin said.

"Forget the news angle," Thor joked. "You just want to see *her*."

"Her" was Lindy Woods, the Satellite News correspondent. She had recently received two outstanding honors. She had been awarded the Pulitzer Prize for Investigative Reporting, and had been named head of the President's Council for Physical Fitness. It was this second achievement that made Lindy Woods so popular. She was often pictured, in magazines and on posters, in a form-fitting tracksuit, competing in the Boston Marathon.

Edward and Laraine Benson already had their wide-screen television tuned in to the Satellite News Network. The boys took seats on the side couch, as the day's events around the world were recounted.

There were two natural catastrophes this time: a flood in China and an earthquake in Hungary. Aid was being sent by the Red Cross. At home, politicians made statements about taxes, minority rights, and getting reelected. A Midwest town managed to get all its citizens to stop smoking for one month and won a large sum of money. In short, it was a typical day in the life of the world, as reported by the news.

". . . .and here's Lindy Woods with her review," said the TV anchorman.

The winsome, light-haired woman came on the air with a story about a new interactive laserdisc video game.

"Biofeedback Fractions!" she exclaimed. "If you happen to try only one game this year, make it this one!"

"Are you listening, Thor?" Mr. Benson chuckled.

"I'm trying to, Dad."

They watched as the reporter placed something resembling a deep-sea diving helmet on her head and sat down on a slowly rotating stand.

"The object is to concentrate on your own alpha-brainwave patterns. Once the machine synchronizes with you, it slowly tries to pull your mind into a beta-wave mode. This is when the action gets difficult."

"Looks like fun," Kevin smiled, as he watched the young woman swirl in the chair.

"You have to maintain your present state of awareness, as *Biofeedback Fractions* suggests others," Lindy said in a voice-over. "There are no words to describe what I am experiencing at this very moment."

The boys watched the procedure closely. After the game stopped, Lindy took off the helmet and spoke directly to the camera again.

"This is something you have to try yourself to believe. It's already available in a few major arcades and will soon be in action around the country. *Biofeedback Fractions,*" she announced. "The latest interactive laser video. For the Satellite News Network, I'm Lindy Woods."

The game started up again and swirled slowly about, as Lindy walked off-camera. Then the weather report came on.

"Nothing new about that," Mr. Benson commented, as he switched off the TV. "Those machines have been used since I was studying at college. Of course, they weren't games then."

Thor refused to get drawn into a discussion with his father over new inventions. In the past, some loud 'differences of opinion' had resulted between Mr. Benson and his son over such statements. To challenge the origin of *Biofeedback Fractions* seemed pointless.

"Well, that's all I wanted to see," Kevin said, as he rose to leave. "How about going to the school tomorrow?"

"During our holidays?" Thor countered.

"We have to get our Science Fair booth approved."

"In that case, come by early."

As Kevin opened the front door, he saw a police car pull up in the Benson's driveway.

"Looks as if Sergeant Dalby is coming in for a coffee," said Thor. "I'm going over to Kevin's."

"No, both of you stay here," Edward told them. "I asked the Sergeant to come by when he had a chance."

The officer gratefully accepted a cup of coffee and relaxed in the living room. He felt as much at ease with these people he had known only two years, as if they'd been lifelong friends. Mr. Benson and Sergeant Dalby had gone on a fishing expedition last summer, and that had solidified a growing friendship.

"I'm sorry for all that confusion," he said. "But those Megadapt people have a high security status. It's out of our hands really."

"The Stanton Police don't have jurisdiction over them?" asked Edward.

"That's a tricky area," admitted the officer. "We got a call from our federal supervisors to do whatever Megadapt requested. You know how it is with anything for the military, Ed."

The man nodded quietly. Thor and Kevin remained puzzled by the power the new company wielded.

"My advice to both of you young fellows is to stay clear of them," Sergeant Dalby concluded.

But Thor protested.

"This whole thing started because of them, sir. It was their people who trespassed here and stole our invention!"

Sergeant Dalby admitted it was a crime. And shrugged.

CHAPTER 6
Random Access Matters

In between classes or after school, many students gathered at the Big Byte. This fast-food restaurant was popular for its large helpings of food and gossip. When someone was starved for a double burger or the latest rumor, the Big Byte satisfied both needs at once.

Sitting in a corner booth, Pamela Powell was recounting yesterday's events to her three girlfriends. They squirmed at the thought of having a police detail block the entrance to a person's own home. Worse, that the police would side with a new company in town against such respected citizens.

"You never know who to trust," said one of the girls.

"My folks say that all the time," added another.

"This could be the only time they're right," joked the first girl.

Pamela took in all their comments with a quiet alertness. She enjoyed the company of these schoolfriends, but found them to be uninterested in matters beyond their immediate concern. Clothes, makeup, parents, and dating absorbed most of their talk.

Kevin and Thor arrived just as the girls were leaving. While the others continued outside, Pam returned to her seat. The boys took a place on each side of her and ordered the Yogurt Shake Special.

"And where were you?" she asked.

"Fixing Mr. Chips," Kevin told her. "All in working order and ready for the school patrol."

"Have to get him mobile for the year," Thor added.

"Aren't you going to miss him?"

"Chips gets visitation rights on the weekend," Thor told her with a chuckle.

The shakes arrived on the table, cool and frothy. Kevin slurped his down in record time, while Thor lingered over the mix with his straw.

"What are you thinking?" Pamela asked him.

Thor shrugged, reluctant to chat. Pam recognized the familiar signs that meant Thor was concentrating deeply on a matter. She felt she had the key to loosen him up.

When he had finished his shake, Pam suggested some fun.

"Let's see if one of those new units is in," she said to the boys.

They left the Big Byte and wandered down the plaza aisle to the Arkade, Stanton's electronic playground. The latest videodisc games stood alongside some dinosaurs of the early ages, such as *Pac-Man* and *Centipede*. The place was relatively quiet today, with about two dozen customers. The trio moved over to the middle-aged attendant who stood against a *TransferTone* game. Kevin got the man's attention.

"Where's *Biofeedback Fractions?*"

"Are you a Lindy Woods fan?" asked the man.

"Sure, why?"

"You must be the twentieth person who's come in here today looking for that game," he stated. "We should be getting one any time. You want to make a reservation?"

The three youths laughed at the suggestion.

"Maybe you won't think it's so funny later," the attendant sneered as he turned away.

They went to the back of the Arkade and took the controls of the famous *Triactor Terrorstorm.* This game was specifically built for three players, each standing on one point of a magnetized triangle. The object was to keep a metal disk levitating over the magnetized floor strip, gradually moving the disk into a higher pattern, until it reached the top of an imaginary pyramid. It required concentration and teamwork, something that the MicroKidz were very good at.

After fifteen minutes of fast action, they let the disk slip and moved onto separate games. Pamela left hers early to stand behind Thor as he played at *WaveLength.*

"When will they get *Starbryte* here?" she asked.

The boy shrugged, continuing to challenge the wave-making patterns of his game.

"*Starbryte* isn't adaptable for arcades," he told her. "Besides, it's still selling okay for home use."

Starbryte was the game program which Thor had developed, with some help from his father. The royalties paid to the youth on the sale of *Starbryte* cartridges came in at a steady rate, but nothing like the windfall after the game first appeared. Thor had earned enough to purchase new equipment, spend the summer at a computer camp, set up his own trust fund for college, and buy a new car. The only problem was that he was too young to get a license until next year. In the meantime, he contributed some gas money to Kevin for his car. The royalties that came in from the home video cartridge now went directly into his bank account. The interest on his savings gave the *Starbryte* inventor enough pocket money so that he didn't need an allowance from his parents.

"I can't wait to try that *Biofeedback* number," Kevin said, when his game ended. "Maybe we should see if they'll take a reservation on it."

"Go ahead," his friend replied.

Thor and Pam watched as the boy walked up to the attendant. They shared a chuckle at Kevin's determination to try the new laserdisc game before anyone else.

"What happens if it's a dud?" wondered Pam.

"He'll send a complaint in to Lindy Woods!"

With a tap on the girl's hand, Thor passed over the control panel of *WaveLength.* Pam demonstrated fast eye-hand coordination on the first three stages, but her skill faded on the upper degrees.

"More practice," she admitted, as the game shut off.

By previous arrangement, Mrs. Powell drove by the plaza to meet the youngsters. She was going in to hold a seminar at the Stanton High School for some visiting student teachers. Since her children and Thor had to get their Science Fair booth plans approved, they had decided to organize a combined trip. Packed into the rear of the station wagon was Mr. Chips.

"You should try to book a space close to the refreshment counter," Mrs. Powell advised.

"Why, Mom?" Pamela inquired. "Kevin will bring his own lunch."

"Not for him, but for everyone else," the woman continued. "At some point, every visitor will stop for something to eat or drink. That means they'll have to pass by your booth. And maybe linger around it."

"They won't be able to do any of that if we don't get the approval from Megadapt to exhibit the Tempest-T," Thor reminded them.

"Go ahead and make your plans regardless," Mrs.

Powell told the trio. "If you keep waiting for others to decide, you'll never accomplish anything."

Her advice made sense. If Willard Stong and Samuel Norse ruled against the youngsters' display, Megadapt Research could find itself the recipient of bad publicity. No company needed such an introduction to its new neighborhood.

The principal agreed to the plans as the three youths presented them. He advised them to secure Megadapt's clearance as soon as possible, to avoid embarrassment. The location near the refreshment counter was granted. This made Kevin particularly happy.

Inside the school's computer room, Mr. Chips was programmed for evening patrol duty. A microchip containing a detailed floor plan with emergency measures was placed into the robot's circuit panel.

"I get the feeling he prefers this to the patrols at home," Kevin commented.

They watched the robot spin, its gyroscope alignment shifting into the patterns required by the new microchip. With a final turn, an indicator light went on. Mr. Chips was in a standby mode for night duty.

The boys began working on some recent data programs, using the school's new Mynd Microcomputer system. The storage and transfer capacity of this unit made all earlier models redundant. By working on it now, Kevin and Thor expected to have an advantage over the rest of the class when school resumed.

In the meantime, Pamela sat in on her mother's seminar. The student teachers, receiving instruction in various approaches to mathematics coaching, ignored the young girl at the back of the class. Pam enjoyed the opportunity to see her mother function in the role she loved. Besides, seeing math explained with the common-sense simplicity which Kay Powell prescribed, gave the girl the secure feeling that everything could be solved, once the right formula was found.

"Who can suggest ways to interest students in theories of pure mathematics?" Mrs. Powell addressed the group.

It was time to step outside, Pam realized. Being a student herself, she felt uncomfortable with this part of the workshop.

"Hey, Pam, in here!"

Walking through the school corridor, she heard Thor Benson calling out from a supply room. With him was her brother, and they were examining a plexiglass display case.

"Want a preview?" Thor offered.

"What is it?"

"An exhibit for the Science Fair. Well, at least half of it. I guess the rest is going to be delivered next week."

The plexiglass case contained a few cards describing the device and process. It was labeled "Fibre-Optic Transducer." One of the cards explained that this unit, when operating, was "*capable of converting energy from one form to another, and making it flow from one or more transmission systems to another*."

"So?" Pam said unimpressed. "What good is it?"

The two boys glanced at each other, smirking. When she did not grasp the science behind a new method immediately, the girl's reaction was always the same. In a word, bored. It took a while for new ideas to sink in, but when they did, Pamela was often capable of making suggestions the original developer had not even considered.

"For one thing," Thor began, "it means that a network

grid of fibre-optic composition, like our cable video and VistaPhone system, becomes two way."

"But we have that already," she said.

"This is different," Kevin said.

The girl peered at the Fibre-Optic Transducer display photographs for a few moments, before coming to her own conclusion.

"Now I see," she smiled. "It can override. This will create two-way systems automatically."

"Well, it has to be connected, first," Thor specified. "If it really can do what these cards describe, this transducer should be a popular exhibit."

Thor had known of many advances which came about because of Science-Fairs. However, he had no way of knowing just how important this exhibit was going to be later on.

Mr. Chips spun around the corner and came through the doorway. On an afternoon patrol circuit, the little robot was rehearsing its surveillance duties.

"He's like a little dog, Thor, follows you everywhere," laughed Pamela.

"But I don't have to feed him. Or clean up the mess."

They watched the robot move over to the wall, stop when its sensors detected the barrier, reverse, and move back out into the hallway.

Mrs. Powell passed by at that moment, nearly running into Mr. Chips.

"We may have to get a license for him," she joked. She saw the trio gathered by the plexiglass display case. "Having a look at your competition?"

"No, Mom, it's our future hope for reverse charges!"

Kevin's comment brought a quick smile to the woman.

"You want a lift home with me, Pam?"

"Sure, Mom. What about the boys?"

"Didn't you get the message from the principal?" Mrs. Powell asked.

"No, what was it?" Kevin inquired.

"Both of you are to be out on the playing field in ten minutes."

"But we don't want to play football," Thor said.

"Neither does the principal," replied the woman.

The instruction sounded odd, she admitted, but the principal was only relaying it from a third party.

"And who is that?" asked Kevin.

When his mother refused to answer, Kevin became more intrigued. Pamela followed her out, and the boys were left alone.

They hurried out onto the football field where the Stanton High School team played its games. The posts stood like guards at each end, overlooking the battles which occurred each Saturday.

"I don't see a thing out here," Kevin said.

"Maybe this is a joke of some kind," Thor wondered.

The noise of an approaching helicopter came out of the northern sky. As the boys watched, it seemed to grow larger. The jet helicopter was circling overhead, lower and lower. Thor and Kevin froze in the center of the playing field as gusts of air swirled like a tornado around them.

The helicopter descended in a thunderous clatter. With its rotors whirling at an invisible rate, the aircraft appeared ready to attack!

CHAPTER 7
The Memory Dump

"Keep low and come forward!"

The voice boomed forth from a speaker alongside the helicopter. Slowly, the boys followed its command and made their way toward it. The churning blades sliced the air above them.

"Hiya, son!"

Edward Benson had shouted from the rear passenger compartment. The words both surprised and comforted Thor.

With Kevin close behind, Thor leaped into the copter's rear section. In a flash, the seatbelts were locked in place. Alongside Mr. Benson was his wife Laraine. Thor grinned at his mother as the helicopter engines shifted to takeoff mode, and the craft soared.

The high school quickly became an anonymous sight. The boys could not discern it from the other numerous low-level buildings that surrounded Stanton.

The pilot waited for the correct altitude before transferring power to his jet engines. A surge ahead caused a sonic boom in their wake, as the dual-charged craft switched into a jet copter.

Watching the countryside whisk by below, Thor had a

chance to collect his thoughts and ask his parents what was going on.

"The convention," reminded Mr. Benson. "We have to make it on time, and this was the only way the company could get us there."

"Which company?"

"Megadapt," Edward replied. "They're sponsoring us and insisted we take you and Kevin along."

"Does my mother know?" Kevin wondered.

"We spoke this morning after Willard Stong made the invitation," Mrs. Benson piped in. "And she packed for you."

Kevin groaned as he saw the green and yellow luggage. He recognized it as the single birthday gift he hated because of its sickly color. He tried not to imagine the choice of clothing made on his behalf.

The landscape changed from rural to suburban, and back again to rural, as the jet copter raced at high speed. Small towns and farm land predominated this part of the country. It was easy for the boys to see how Stanton was just another dot on the earth, made important only by the recent movement of so many major high-tech industries from the city.

In a short while, skyscrapers were seen looming up from the horizon.

Approaching the city from the north, the pilot settled into a flight corridor bringing them into the heart of the metropolis. The jet propulsion was switched off as the craft returned to its auxiliary engines. As the four passengers held their breath, office buildings passed by so closely that people inside waved from their desks.

The surrounding towers rose higher. Thor and Kevin looked out to see the landing port draw near. A wide phosphorescent circle was the target. When the pilot expertly touched down, three flight deck personnel rushed from a small shelter to latch tight the wheels. As the rotors came to a winding halt, the passengers disembarked.

The boys hurried to the edge of the skyscraper. A wire fence bordered the landing zone. They gazed at the streets sixty stories below. Tiny trucks and cars moved in the perpetual traffic jam which characterized the city. By the time its noise ascended to this height, the sounds were muffled by winds carrying it out to sea.

"Over this way," shouted one of the attendants.

They boarded an elevator near the rooftop shelter. Moments later, the Benson family and Kevin Powell hurtled to the ground in a steel-mirrored rapid elevator. Their ears popped twice along the way, but everyone knew to yawn and relieve the pressure.

"Mr. Benson, would you come this way?"

A hotel clerk greeted the family and led them into the foyer. Visitors from all over the world, in many styles of dress and speaking many languages, moved through the hotel lobby. While her husband checked in at the main desk, Mrs. Benson took the youths aside.

"You'll need some of this," she said, handing a brown envelope to her son. "Divide it between yourselves, but try to make it last until we leave."

"Spending money is not meant to be saved," Thor smiled.

"Nor all spent in one day," she reminded.

Mr. Benson returned to the group and handed a room key to Thor.

"You're both staying across the hall from us. Now your mother and I will be going upstairs to get cleaned up. Not that I need to, but you know how fussy she is," he said, as Laraine gave him a playful nudge. "In the meantime, stroll around. But be back in an hour. We still have to register at the convention office."

With the money envelope secure in his pocket, Thor walked with Kevin out the front doors of the hotel.

The boys immediately noticed the smells of the metropolis around them. They had been breathing fresh country air for so long, the smoggy environment came as a shock to them. They were thankful their stay was to be a short one.

Strolling through the busy streets, the boys wondered why so many pedestrians were out during these peak office hours. Perhaps many companies here were on Flextime, Kevin suggested, meaning it was the workers themselves who decided what their working hours would be.

"And just imagine the large number of people who work from their homes transmitting computerized data to other personal centres," Thor added.

One event they always loved in the city was visiting the video arcades for a look at what was new on the market. They found one such outlet on a side street, where a sign in front flashed "VIDEORAMA".

Fifty customers played at a variety of games. Thor reached into his pocket and divided the money with his friend.

"Let's get a token each and try to outrun the machine," he suggested.

"And the first one to lose buys the next round."

One player was playing the air bubble game *Extractor*. It was a fully enclosed contraption that was suspended and rolled in midair by a stream of vapor. They watched the player fly the floating bubble with expert ease. It did not seem to be the challenge it was just months ago.

"Hey, there it is!" Thor declared. "*Biofeedback Fractions*!"

A group of people were standing around the machine seen on the Satellite News report. They waited curiously for someone to demonstrate its action.

"I have to try this for Lindy's sake," murmured Kevin.

"You're not at all intrigued by this yourself, are you Kev?" teased Thor.

The youths took up places at the two playing pods. The helmets were pulled on, the tokens inserted, and the stand slowly rotated.

Each player concentrated on his own alpha-brainwave pattern, as it magically appeared in his mind's eye. As the machine began to synchronize, it started shifting into a beta-wave mode.

Thor gripped his hand straps tightly. Suddenly, wild images blazed across Thor's consciousness: images of wild horses, exploding automobiles, endless deserts, faces of a hundred thousand people, buildings sprouting from the earth like mushrooms, supernovas frozen in space, and a flurry of others. Nightmares and daydreams became one. Gradually, he managed to slow the action to a standstill.

Thor Benson believed he had outrun *Biofeedback Fractions*, until he removed his helmet. He then discovered that the machine had called him "OUT" prior to achieving the final three thresholds.

"So here's a game that's really a challenge," he thought to himself. "But once a day is enough. Any more, and my circuits might overload."

The greater surprise was Kevin Powell. He was still playing the game. According to the external register, he was lingering inside the final threshold.

Other spectators asked Thor about what had occurred,

but he was directing his full attention to the other pod. Kevin seemed to be toying with the new interactive laserdisc game.

"When is he going to quit?" Thor began to worry.

Without looking at the register, Thor reached out and shook Kevin's back. Suddenly, the threshold indicator peaked and froze. Kevin went rigid.

Panic drove Thor to tear away the helmet from his friend's head. The images from the powerful mind game had etched themselves into Kevin's expression.

"Why did you ruin that?" was all he managed to say.

Thor assisted him from the playing pod. Another youngster hurried to replace Kevin, hoping to achieve the same threshold response.

"It only felt like it went on for a minute," Kevin mumbled, as they left the Videorama arcade.

"But you were in there nearly forty minutes! A lot longer than me. What were you seeing?"

Kevin returned a blissful smile, as if holding onto a new-found inner secret. His reaction mystified Thor.

The action and aftereffects of *Biofeedback Fractions* dwelt in Thor's thoughts. One lingering image was that of a three-dimensional brain, electrical charges flowing through its contours. What did it mean?

The boys made their way along the crowded sidewalk. They stopped for a giant hot dog with the works, served up by a street vendor. Munching this quick lunch would save them from having to dine out with the adults, leaving more time for touring the convention displays.

In the hotel lobby, Mr. Benson pinned identification badges to their shirts.

"This gets you into all the seminars, workshops, and equipment demonstrations," he told them. "You're free to see whatever you want. But don't leave the area. Now, about lunch . . ."

"Taken care of," interjected Thor.

Kevin smiled at how his friend had foreseen his parents' suggestion.

They agreed to meet later that day for dinner, and to recount details of convention activities. Mr. Benson reminded Thor that the speech on behalf of his consulting firm had been rescheduled for a later time than the program indicated.

As the boys drifted over to the exhibition floor, they noticed an array of television lights by the entrance.

"I bet that's Satellite News," Thor stated.

"And there's my dreamgirl!" declared Kevin.

A small crowd had gathered at the edge of the scene, out of camera range, to watch the interview in progress. Both boys thought that Lindy Woods was even more sleek and magnetic in person than on TV. Two men were being interviewed. One of them was an interpreter, translating for the other.

"The translator," whispered Thor.

"What about him?"

"Doesn't he look familiar?"

Kevin studied the man before replying, "Not really."

"He reminds me of someone at Megadapt," Thor told him.

The boys squeezed in closer to hear the translation taking place. They couldn't hear everything, but certain key words hung in the air: "Identical to fingerprints . . . scattered signals . . . unique to each person . . . brainwaves . . . biofeedback . . . playing games . . . ," caught their attention.

The interview concluded with Lindy Woods facing the camera for a wrap-up. "And our congratulations to Dr.

Fuentes on his dynamic contributions to modern science."

At that point, the television lights dimmed, and two other men stepped from the side. Thor and Kevin were brushed along by these security agents who escorted Dr. Fuentes and his interpreter to a waiting elevator.

"Who does he think he is?" Kevin spouted, after one of the agents stepped on his foot.

Thor Benson intended to find out.

"Excuse me, but aren't you Lindy Woods?" Thor raised his voice, as a cameraman moved near the woman.

She smiled, beckoning him on.

"My friend here would like to meet you," continued Thor. "He's sort of shy."

In fast order, Thor had prodded the surprised youth towards the famous reporter. Kevin turned a few shades of red, embarrassed at this sudden introduction to his favorite media personality.

Lindy Woods looked amused at these anxious youngsters stepping over the cables to meet her. When he drew close, Thor surprised her by not asking something personal.

"That man you just interviewed," he blurted.

"Dr. Fuentes?"

"No, his interpreter," Thor clarified.

Her puzzled reaction was apparent as she scrutinized the boys.

"Why would you be more interested in a translator?" she asked. Then, in an offhand way, remarked, "It's certainly not what I expected. I thought your friend wanted an autograph."

"Oh, but I do!" Kevin declared.

Lindy scribbled her name on a photo handed her by one of the Satellite News production assistants.

"We took your suggestion," Kevin said nervously.

"Pardon me?"

"Playing the *Biofeedback Fractions* game," explained Thor.

"What did you think?" she asked.

"I love it," Kevin replied, entranced by the woman.

"It scared me," Thor said.

"Just how I felt," she confessed. "But as for the name of that translator, maybe you could find out through Dr. Fuentes's sponsor."

Another assistant came up to the reporter with details about the next interview. The boys stepped back with a wave of appreciation.

"Let's find out who this Dr. Fuentes is," Kevin suggested.

People drifted across the convention floor and passed into the exhibition rooms. Many clutched bright blue and red folders. Stamped on the side of them, in gold lettering, was the company name and logo for Megadapt.

"They sure seem to be everywhere," the boys thought.

A directory listed the speakers for each section. Thor noted his father's name in the middle of the list and put a check mark beside it. They scanned down through the rest of the list to the second last name.

"Dr. Hector Fuentes, Ph.D., University of Balkat, this evening at 7 P.M."

"Maybe we'll bump into him somewhere before that," Thor said. "Or the man speaking for him."

Turning now to enter the exhibition area, the boys presented their ID badges to a guard. He fed these cards through a portable Q-D-Tector. Once its green light flashed, the boys were permitted entry. These special security measures were imposed to restrict illegal or unwanted individuals from obtaining classified high-tech data.

Sections of the exhibition area were devoted to recent scientific discoveries in diverse areas. Among the most prominent were Biogenetics, Education, Health, Research and Development, Military, Transportation, Government and—most intriguing to the boys—Experimentals.

Fifteen booths comprised the Experimentals section. Each was staffed by at least three attendants to explain the variety of displays. Some of these companies were recognized for their expertise in other fields. Many were fresh from a university laboratory and into the business marketplace for the first time. Then there was Alpha-Better.

"Wow!" exclaimed Kevin.

"Hold everything," whispered Thor.

What had caught their attention was a rotating holographic display. Hovering in midair, with light radiating from inside, was a realistic 3-D image of the human brain! The neuron and synapse system glowed as a light pattern followed the charged action—of a thought?—through the brain. After watching the procedure repeated, Kevin and Thor approached one of the Alpha-Better attendants.

"What is Alpha-Better?" inquired Thor.

"A research company," replied the attendant. "We collect data to translate, assemble, and market."

Kevin, meanwhile, was examining the 3-D image.

"What's the origin of this model?" he asked.

"Our laboratory. This is just a demonstration unit, but the possibilities are limitless."

Thor had his own interest. "Is this a hologram of an actual brain, or a computer-generated graphic?"

"In a way, both," came the odd response. "It evolved from studies done by one of our foreign subsidiaries."

"Can you really trace the electrical flow through the synapses?" Kevin asked.

The attendant invited the youths to step back into the display area. The Alpha-Better exhibit did not seem as luxuriously furnished as some of the others, but it did have a unique stock of microprocessors.

"We can monitor thoughts in action," she claimed, tapping a circular box mounted on one of the graphics display monitors.

"I doubt that," snickered Kevin.

It was a dare. He accepted her invitation to try a demonstration. The attendant fitted a familiar-looking helmet onto the boy. Thor watched uneasily from the side.

"I'll describe all the methods that . . ."

Her voice faded, as the microprocessors pulsed into action.

Kevin Powell remembered nothing more. He had the feeling of slipping into unconsciousness.

CHAPTER 8
Dispersed Intelligence

"Are you all right?"

The ceiling lights came into focus. Kevin felt Thor leaning close to him and tapping his shoulder.

"Can you hear me, Kev?"

All Kevin could manage in response was a groggy mumble. He shook his head and glanced beyond his friend. The attendants from the Alpha-Better exhibit stood behind, observing closely.

"What happened?"

"You drifted off on us," the woman attendant replied. "For a moment, we thought of charging you a hotel fee," she added, in an attempt to make light of the ordeal.

"Your friend probably had too much excitement earlier," said someone else. "And maybe too much for lunch."

Thor disregarded their comments and helped Kevin from the chair. He managed to stand upright, but still felt weary. Thor led him to a refreshment area and ordered two large protein milkshakes. As the boys sat sipping them, the cobwebs began to leave Kevin's head.

"How long was I out?"

"Maybe ten minutes."

"What did they do?"

"At first nothing," Thor said. "And I thought everything was normal. Then they switched on that processor above the monitor."

"What did it show?"

"Are you ready for this?" Thor asked carefully. "If I didn't know you, I'd say it was your thought patterns. I didn't believe it myself at first, but I overheard them whispering, as they recorded it on that little MindPrinter."

"What?" Kevin asked, startled.

Together, the youths decided to begin a private inquiry into the Alpha-Better Company. Surely Mr. Benson would be able to assist them.

Unfortunately, neither Mr. nor Mrs. Benson could be contacted. The electronic paging device, which his father always carried, did not respond to their "Alert" signal.

"Maybe they're swimming," suggested Kevin.

Instead of returning to their room, the boys decided to continue their tour of the exhibition hall. Thor was in a lighthearted mood and hinted that Kevin again offer himself as a demonstration model.

"I'm not a good guinea pig," admitted Thor.

Knowing that his mother was always on the lookout for innovations, Kevin made a side trip to the Education displays.

Various videotext publishers were handing out free samples of hard-copy printouts. Methods for dealing with learning disabled youngsters were available on video cassettes. School Attendance Forms and Truancy Response Telephone Dialers did a good business. Automatic teaching aids, controlled from a centralized mainframe computer, drew large crowds.

The youths walked through, collecting sample kits.

They were caught in the movement toward a familiar red logo.

"Alpha-Better Teaching Methods," Thor whispered in astonishment.

"Maybe they're using the research from Experimentals in the school system," Kevin theorized.

As they advanced to the booth, the boys caught sight of the two attendants they'd met in the other section. The man and woman were now explaining the use of a micromonitoring device.

"Let's get Dad," Thor said. "Okay, Kev?"

But Kevin was no longer standing beside him!

Frantically, Thor looked for him above the heads of the crowd. He didn't want to attract attention, so he refrained from calling aloud. Pushing his way to the edge of the throng, Thor at last saw Kevin. He was standing beside the mysterious translator and Dr. Fuentes!

They seemed to be having a close conversation, so Thor decided to watch from behind two delegates standing in the middle of the aisle. A few moments later, Kevin saw him peering about. With a wave, he indicated that Thor should join them.

"So you also saw the Alpha-Better Thought Scanner," the interpreter said to Thor.

"I already explained," grinned Kevin.

"Yes," Thor offered. "But what does Dr. Fuentes know of it?"

The others, including Kevin, had a brief chuckle.

"He invented it!" Kevin revealed.

"And from what your friend tells us, he made quite an impression," the interpreter stated. "In fact, he overloaded some microcircuits."

"He did?" Thor asked.

"That is why the Doctor and myself were called down

from our suite," explained the interpreter. "And the two people from our Experimentals branch had to be transferred here."

The events that occurred now came in such quick succession, that the boys would ask themselves later if it all really did take place.

Kevin's voice came over the speaker system at the Alpha-Better Teaching Methods booth.

"What's going on?" he asked, stunned by this development.

His friend shrugged, peering over to the activity in front of the booth.

Dr. Fuentes and the translator were now standing on the platform beside the booming speakers.

Kevin's voice rolled over the audience. "What's the origin of this model? . . . Can you really trace the electrical flow through the synapses? . . . I doubt that!"

They were the exact words Kevin had spoken before he fell unconscious.

Incredibly, a 3-D image of a human brain floated in the air. The boy's words were repeated. By the action of this strange hologram, it seemed that the voice and 3-D image were interconnected!

"How did they get that?" Kevin was terrified.

Dr. Fuentes spoke in his native language, as his associate translated. He referred to the MindPrinter used at the other booth. Its use in educational systems was declared. Most significantly, he described its capacity for picking out thoughts from any student undergoing a test.

"In a manner of speaking, intelligence and learning abilities are known without external quizzes, tests, or exams. We can take the scattered signals among a multitude of brainwaves, break them down, and translate them back into speech patterns unique to that person," concluded the interpreter.

The crowd fell into a hush. Such an invention had extraordinary potential. And not just for educational purposes.

"What about its military use?"

The question was raised by a man at the front of the gathering.

The translator relayed the question to Dr. Fuentes, who scoffed at it.

"Dr. Fuentes and his government pledge world peace. There are, therefore, no military applications for his devices," stated the translator. "This MindPrinter is solely used for educational research and assisting young students."

"Right," the man in the audience said. "And Dr. Fuentes has no such computer-aided designs for the military?"

The translator scowled. "Next question, please!"

The man pushed his way to the aisle and headed toward an exit. Two burly men, the same pair who had escorted Dr. Fuentes and the interpreter following the Satellite News Network interview, trailed the man who had dared to question.

"I don't like what's going on," Thor whispered.

"Time for a break," agreed Kevin. "We should get in touch with your folks and find out who this Dr. Fuentes is."

At the Alpha-Better exhibit, people were pressed solidly together, as the MindPrinter and its originator came under more scrutiny. Suddenly, in the midst of the barrage of questions, a warning was shouted. The MindPrinter and 3-D laser projection unit crashed to the floor!

Sparks flew from the scattered electronic pieces and

pandemonium set in. From nearby, Thor and Kevin watched a fight erupt. The exhibit booth was knocked apart. Possibly a dozen men, and several women, were in the free-for-all battle involving fists, chairs, and karate.

Sirens wailed as alarms were set off. Attendants at other exhibits immediately drew curtains or pulled back expensive displays, in case the violence spread. Specially clad security officers rushed to the disturbance.

Curious at what might happen next, the youths moved closer. The battle was in full swing.

"Kevin! Thor!"

They turned to see Edward and Laraine Benson on the far side of the hall. The parents pointed toward a side door. Pushing through the mob, they all reached an emergency exit. They raced out and along a back corridor and down some steps that led onto a fire escape ladder.

"Sorry to cut short this visit," Mr. Benson told them, "but I'm cancelling out of this mess."

"Just as it's getting exciting," Thor smirked.

"Any more excitement, and I'll have more gray hairs than I have hair!" the man stated.

A walk through the rear passageway brought them onto a side street. The Bensons and Kevin made their way to the front of the hotel. By this time, a fleet of police vehicles had blockaded the entrance.

The air was split open with the screech of sirens. Burly officers ran in and out of the hotel. Culprits from the convention floor battle were hustled into waiting paddy wagons. Throngs of spectators, mainly shoppers and office workers attracted by the sirens, gathered across the street.

As his father moved toward a small group of observers, Thor imagined the confusion and destruction still taking place inside. Mrs. Benson and Kevin pulled him along, as Mr. Benson approached a familiar gentleman on the sidewalk.

"I was wondering whether we'd meet today," said Mr. Benson.

"Hello, Edward." Willard Stong, wearing his Compu-Blindsight glasses smiled at the man. "Rather upsetting way to spend the afternoon, isn't it?"

"I could think of better ways," came the reply.

"At least the boys are safe," Willard smiled. "It was a concern that they might be too close when the—ah—diversion began."

"You knew this was going to happen," Thor surmised.

"It was all planned?" Kevin asked, astonished.

Willard Stong wouldn't confirm Megadapt's role in the sudden eruption. He turned to face the hotel entrance, as a cheer went up from some spectators watching a new group of captives being escorted to a police van.

"It was only a matter of time," mumbled Willard Stong.

The targets of the crowd's jeers emerged from the hotel. Surrounded by four policemen, were the translator and Dr. Fuentes, in handcuffs!

CHAPTER 9
Readapting

That evening, the Megadapt jet helicopter carried a tired group back to Stanton. The lights of the city twinkled into darkness as the craft hurtled over the countryside.

The day's events were recounted in a lengthy discussion with Willard Stong. A number of strange occurrences seemed linked in some way to the family, but the pieces did not fit together.

Kevin Powell sat quietly in the rear compartment. He reviewed his own role in the confusion. The *Biofeedback Fractions* arcade game brought good memories to mind. However, his experience with the Thought Scanner and MindPrinter was most unsettling. Who was Dr. Fuentes really developing the Alpha-Better Teaching Methods for? What became of the brain imprint which he had left? Some of the wild images from the new interactive laser-disc game reappeared in his thoughts.

"She's responsible for getting me to try it," he thought, looking down at his autographed photo of Lindy Woods. "Maybe she can help in answering some of these questions." He folded the picture and put it back in his pocket, determined to speak to Lindy Woods again.

"I saw you on the news!" was Pamela's greeting when he arrived home.

"What?"

"You were on the Satellite News," she told him. "And guess who the reporter was?"

Kevin already knew it was his favorite, the woman whose photo he carried.

"We couldn't see you clearly at first," Mrs. Powell broke in, "but when we played the tape back and slowed it down, we saw you and Thor standing at the edge of the screen."

"How did it all start?" Pamela asked.

Not wanting to alarm his mother, Kevin gave an undramatic account of the day. He described the scene inside the hall leading up to the disturbance. Details concerning the Thought Scanner and MindPrinter were best left for another time, he decided.

While a hot microwaved delicacy was set before him, Kevin stared at the room's video monitor. Pamela rewound the tape, and the image of Lindy Woods came to life.

The interview with Dr. Fuentes was reduced to a twenty second summary. Lindy spoke of her understanding of the scientist's main achievement. Next, a camera shot, probably from one of the security monitors above the exhibition hall, showed the melee beginning. In the outside segment, where the combatants were led to the police vans, the camera showed the crowd gathering. There, in plain view once the picture was held in stop-motion, were Kevin, the Bensons and Willard Stong.

"I hope that isn't noted by the wrong people," he muttered.

"You know where the Satellite News goes," his sister reminded. "Everywhere on earth."

Kevin gulped his meal with the usual haste. The talk around him went by unheard. He only paid attention to his mother again when she suggested they subscribe to a home security service.

"With the state things are in, it might be wise for us," said the woman.

"Don't worry, Mom," Kevin told her. "I'll get Mr. Chips off his night duty and bring him here."

"Not that little trashcan," snorted Pam. "I'd get the woozies. All his clattering and sneaking around."

"He says nice things about you," Kevin chortled.

"I thought Thor gave it on loan to the school," his mother said.

"That was just for reorientation," he explained. "Chips is supposed to be on patrol during the preparation of the Science Fair. That's still a few days away."

The next morning, Kevin called his friend over to view the taped Satellite News report. As a result, Thor suggested they contact Lindy Woods to get a transcript of the unused interview with Dr. Fuentes.

"I'll take any excuse you have to give her a call," Kevin joked.

Edward Benson waited for his son and Kevin in the driveway. At Thor's urging, he had decided to search out information on Dr. Fuentes and the Alpha-Better connection. After two blasts of his car horn, the boys hurried out to join him for the drive to his midtown Stanton office.

Like most electronic data consultants, Mr. Benson's work area was equipped with the latest computer hardware. As an expert technician, he also used a number of experimental prototypes. These were the machines that most interested Thor.

Using his private password code, Mr. Benson logged

on to a confidential government database. His mainframe addressed the Immigration Entry file.

"DR. HECTOR FUENTES, GRANTED TEMPORARY VISA FOR SIX MONTHS, NOW ON SECOND EXTENSION," the display monitor reported. "NO RESTRICTIONS. SPONSORED BY THE ALPHA-BETTER CORPORATION."

"That's pretty straightforward," commented Mr. Benson.

The two boys nodded silently.

"Now for the Corporation enquiry," he said.

The listing for the Alpha-Better head office was not entered in any database! Mr. Benson failed to draw out even the Company's Taxation Reports. Only one piece of information could be obtained.

"THE CHARTER FOR THIS CORPORATION IS HELD BY A PRIVATE COMPANY," they noted from the computer report. "FOR SECURITY PURPOSES, ALL DATA IS OFF-LINE. SUPREME LEVEL CLEARANCE ONLY."

Mr. Benson shook his head in resignation.

"That means presidential use only, no others need apply," he remarked.

"So that's a dead end?" asked Kevin.

"At least through this," Mr. Benson declared, tapping the top of the display monitor. "The company certainly does have a top security rating. And since Dr. Fuentes is sponsored by them, he must be a valuable asset."

The two boys left the office disappointed. Even with the assistance of Mr. Benson's computing power, they could not pierce the mystery.

At Stanton High School, the half-day schedule was in effect. This system of timetables needed adjusting when first introduced, but now clearly proved superior to the old standard of five full days per week.

An availability of outside resources had made the change essential. Since the town housed so many research and development firms, part of the education process took place on the job. Not only were the schools and teachers benefiting, but the youngsters themselves found ready employment opportunities upon graduation. Those students not working with a specific firm had the option of visiting other schools and junior colleges to use their facilities.

"Hey, that was some riot!"

"You sure picked a fine hotel!"

"What was the jet copter like?"

"Who caused the fight in the first place?"

Nearly everybody at school seemed aware of the boys' adventure. Most were more interested in details of the disturbance than in hearing about the technical displays.

After awhile, Thor and Kevin ignored most of the questions. They attended two classes, prepared notes for future assignments, and retreated to the school's Compu-Room.

"I thought it wasn't going to end!" said Kevin in disgust. "Why are people so fascinated with violence?"

"Must be our caveman instinct," Thor mused.

"More like an amoeba's," added his friend. "Oh, I almost forgot. How about getting Mr. Chips out tonight? My Mom would rest a lot easier if he was on patrol at our house."

They went to the principal's office, where the release was granted. The boys agreed to return their robot for night duty prior to the Science Fair.

"Look at this," smiled Kevin. "A mechanical ad!"

Taped to the front of the two-foot tall robot was a poster advertising the upcoming Science Fair. As they escorted

Mr. Chips down the hall, they considered other entries to submit.

"But they'd take months," Thor concluded with a groan. "We'll have to call Mr. Norse to clear the Tempest-T for that weekend."

"And if they don't agree, we'll build an identical one!"

"There's only one set of plans," Thor reminded him.

"Where are they?"

Thor touched his head. The secrets of the Tempest-T microassembly were safe in his mind.

Either way, the boys would manage. If Megadapt was worried, then the company should provide its own security guards. It had enough of them, with a few Doberman pinschers along, to give any thieves second thoughts.

Kevin and Thor were packing Mr. Chips into the back of the Powell's station wagon when Pamela came out of the school with two of her girlfriends. Thor and Kevin said hello but weren't interested in socializing. They had important work to do.

"Mom said you can drive it back," Pam announced, as she handed her brother the keys. "But first you have to drop us off at the Big Byte. Okay?"

Kevin couldn't resist. The thick sandwiches and frothy shakes were tempting, as was the opportunity to look over the opposite sex.

On the drive over, Pamela's friends insisted on playing a compact disk on the car's quad speakers at full volume. No one seemed to mind; after all it was the latest release by The Random Accessories.

Just parking in front of the Big Byte gave Kevin hunger pains.

"Only one of the Specials," Kevin promised.

The two boys and three girls filled their round table

with snacks and drinks. No race was declared, but one seemed to be in effect. As usual, Kevin won.

"What are you doing later?" Pam asked.

"Going to set up Mr. Chips," replied her brother.

"And you, Thor?" she wondered, in a voice to make her girlfriends jealous.

"I'll give Kevin a hand. And then wait for you."

It was the answer she wanted the others to hear. The girls glanced enviously at Pamela.

When the boys returned to the car, Kevin chided Thor for the cute comment.

"Better watch what you say to my sister. She already has a crush on you."

"Oh, yeah?" mumbled Thor.

"The size of a football field!"

The sight of someone coming out of the Arkade nearby brought another memory to Kevin. He left his friend standing outside, as he hurried over. The attendant stood inside the doorway of the games palace.

"*Biofeedback Fractions*?" Kevin inquired.

"Any day now," replied the bored man. "You kids are all the same!"

Kevin ran back to the car where Thor waited.

"It still isn't here."

"But you've played it already."

"And did real fine, too," Kevin mentioned.

"After your blackout on the Alpha-Better Thought Scanner, you should cool anything to do with mind taps."

"Maybe, but there are some wild images that came up, and I'd like to capture them again," Kevin declared.

Silently, Thor considered another possible reason for his friend's determination. Was there a link?

They returned to Matrix Boulevard. Mr. Chips was carried into the Powell home and placed in the front room. While Kevin rummaged in his own workshop, Thor adjusted the robot's wheels. He used a special wire chain, actually an old bicycle chain, to allow the patrolling unit to raise and lower itself on the staircase.

Kevin reappeared with a compact case. Thor began unscrewing the top of the robot.

"Good thing I found it," he said, holding the microchip. "Sure beats having to set up another program."

The entire floor plan, electrical system, and communications insert plugs of the Powell house were implanted on the tiny semiconductor. Mr. Chips had an inbuilt heat-sensor unit, which enabled him to detect any human present by the registration of their specific body heat. When the reaction was positive, Mr. Chips set off an alarm that contacted the Stanton Police.

"Sure beats having a guard dog," Thor said.

"At least he won't fall asleep on a hot day," added Kevin.

The microchip was plugged into the "brains" of the robot.

With a tap on the rear control panel, Mr. Chips began his cruise. The heat-sensor device would not be activated until the house was vacated.

As a test, Kevin pressed the number sequence to order "UPSTAIRS PATROL." End over end, the metal chain lifted the wheels. Mr. Chips mounted the stairway easily. The boys followed its tour of the halls and bedrooms.

When the telephone rang, Mr. Chips intercepted the call. Kevin quickly pressed the override button, and the caller's voice came through the robot's speaker. It was Mrs. Benson.

"If Thor is there, could you ask him to come over, please?"

"On my way, Mom," he replied into the microphone.

Kevin decided to stay home.

"I'll stick around here. May as well get some homework out of the way."

As Thor headed home, he saw the black car parked in his parent's driveway.

"Oh, give me a break," he muttered, spotting the Megadapt parking sticker on the front window.

Samuel Norse was seated in the living room. Mrs. Benson appeared relaxed and smiling, as if a joke had just been shared.

"How are you, Mr. Norse?"

"As well as you," he smiled at Thor. "I've been working with your father today. We've hired him as a special consultant."

Thor wondered why he had to be called over to hear this. Surely the subject would be discussed over dinner.

"Great," he managed to say.

"Tell me, why haven't you been assigned to any high-tech firm for this semester?" the man asked.

"I'm doing my own research. At least I was, until your people took it away."

"Ah, the Tempest-T," he smiled. "You can rest assured that it will be working for your Science Fair."

This brought a smile to the boy.

"In the meantime, and your mother approves of this, we at Megadapt Research would like you to come on board with us."

"No kidding?"

"You'll have access to our research labs, experimental sections, and anything else Megadapt can provide."

The opportunity was incredibly tempting.

"What about Kevin?"

Mr. Norse paused and looked over at Mrs. Benson. She had probably warned the man of her son's reaction.

"I'm sorry. This is a single placement only. We simply don't require another student."

The official decision was plain. Thor stood motionless as he considered working without his best friend and science cohort. The boys had grown up together, helping each other out of many difficulties and always sharing an eager sense of discovery.

"But I do my best work with him," explained Thor. "His mother was my first math systems teacher. We've always been partners."

"It's just not possible."

Mrs. Benson tried to indicate with a steady gaze that Thor accept the condition.

"Just for this semester," she said.

Thor thought the matter through.

"No thanks."

CHAPTER 10
Data Link

Pamela Powell returned home to find Mr. Chips patrolling the front yard. The robot tracked along the entrance walkway, stopped, circled, and returned to the side door. Its heat detectors responded to the girl's presence.

"Who is that?" Mr. Chips's metallic voice asked.

A set of speech loops had been prerecorded to play through its speaker system at the appropriate time.

"Good day, Mr. Chips," Pam said in return.

"Friendly voice," analyzed the machine.

"And how's your bucket of bolts?" she added sarcastically.

The robot was left speechless. No response to this was available.

The home security system was deactivated when Mr. Chips recognized her familiar speech pattern. Pamela knew this procedure only too well. One time, she had returned with a girlfriend, who had replied to the robot. As a result, Mr. Chips secretly alerted the Stanton Police desk. The girls were in the kitchen when they found themselves raided by two officers. Mr. Chips had proved his worth, and Pamela had learned her lesson.

"Anybody home?" she called out.

Silence greeted her. As Pam crossed the hallway, she noticed a blinking light atop the PIRX printer. A message was awaiting transfer. Probably another memo from Thor to her brother, she thought, clicking the machine into RUN.

The swirling waters in the Jacuzzi whirlpool soothed the tension caused by her tennis game. Pam replayed the shots in her mind, hoping to avoid the same mistakes next time. A towel draped over her hair, she walked back to the kitchen in a housecoat.

She tore the newly printed message from the tractor feeder and placed it on Kevin's chair.

An hour later, while pouring herself a glass of apple juice she looked more closely at the form.

"PRIVATE & CONFIDENTIAL," it began.

Pamela could not resist reading the rest.

"SPECIAL FOR KEVIN POWELL," continued the telecopy. "FROM SATELLITE NEWS REPORTER LINDY WOODS."

"Incredible," grinned Pam.

She read the message three times, noting each reference to her brother. The sign-off and modem return code seemed authentic. Now that Kevin was part of a developing news story, Pam wanted to be involved. But the restraining words "PRIVATE & CONFIDENTIAL" made her stop and think.

Should she tell Thor? They were all best friends, but wasn't she duty-bound to get this data to Kevin first?

"When did Chips get here?" asked Mrs. Powell, as she entered carrying her briefcase. "He popped out of the bushes and gave me a shock."

Kay Powell was distracted while removing her coat and did not see the PIRX page Pam slid under a placemat.

"He was here when I came in, too," replied Pam.

"And where's Kevin?"

"That's what I'd like to know!"

"What do you mean?" she asked, noting her daughter's anxiousness.

"Nothing, Mom, just wondering. Like you are."

She gave the girl a sideways glance, sensing, in that special way parents have, that something was going on, but knowing she shouldn't push. She knew the matter would soon surface, and Pam would tell her about it when she was ready.

"I was in the principal's office for an hour after classes ended. That's why I'm late," she said. "They need volunteer help for the Science Fair. So I volunteered you."

"Why?" protested the girl. "Volunteers offer themselves. They can't be forced in."

"I'm asking you, Pam. It's only right that you contribute to the organization."

The familiar screeching of car brakes in the driveway announced Kevin's return. Pam lit up as he came through the door.

"Hey, Kev! Want to know who . . . ?"

Pamela stopped when she saw Thor entering right behind her brother.

"What?" Kevin asked.

"Tell ya later," she said, then left the room.

Mrs. Powell shrugged, as Kevin and Thor looked to her.

"Did I do something wrong?" wondered Kevin.

"Maybe it was me," muttered Thor.

"No, she was that way when I came in earlier," the woman assured them. "And she's upset at being volunteered to assist at the Science Fair."

"But Pam's working with us," Thor stated.

"Does she know that?" asked the surprised mother.

"No, we were going to ask," Kevin broke in. Then, shouting toward his sister's room, "Hey, Pammy, wanna help at our exhibit?"

Seconds later, the girl emerged with a huge smile on her face. She sat down at the table where her glass of apple juice had remained. With a calculating look, she spoke to the boys.

"On one condition," she stated.

"Say it."

"Promise to introduce me to Lindy Woods!"

A piercing look passed between brother and sister. There was no doubt in Kevin's mind that Pam had intercepted a return message from the reporter.

Kevin changed the subject. "Let's get that electron-scope in my workroom," he said to Thor, wanting to forestall any other mention of Lindy Woods.

While Mrs. Powell was busy in the living room, Pam lingered in her own quarters. Music hummed through a hanging speaker ball above her bed. A video monitor was tuned to a replay of a school lecture. She paid attention to neither. Her wait ended with a tap on her door.

Kevin entered. She pulled the PIRX printout from a drawer. He took it without speaking and sat down in a chair to read it.

"You didn't show this to Mom?" Kevin checked.

"Not when it said 'PRIVATE AND CONFIDENTIAL'," stated Pam.

"And promise me you won't tell any of your girlfriends!"

Just then, they heard a scraping sound against the door. In a swift move, Kevin leapt up and pulled open the door.

"Mr. Chips," Pam uttered in relief.

The little robot proceeded into the room, circled, and

then left. It stopped at the door, its indicator light flashing.

"What's the matter?" asked Pam.

"Probably tired after climbing the stairs. Or he's drained a solar battery."

As the boy bent over the unit, he heard voices from the front door area. His mother was speaking with Mrs. Benson and Thor in an unusually loud, argumentative voice. Creeping along the hallway for a better vantage point, he heard the final phrase.

". . . . then talk to your son, Kay, and clear it up!"

The door closed, and silence returned. Kevin indicated that Pam should join him, and they went to the kitchen together.

"Did you ask Thor not to take his work semester at Megadapt?" Mrs. Powell demanded when Kevin entered.

"No. Why?"

"Laraine and Edward think you've influenced him."

Kevin was surprised by the misunderstanding.

"He told me nothing about an offer, Mom, honest. And if he did get one, I'd tell him to take it."

"He said he'd only take the job on the condition that you were hired as well."

"He did? That's no reason to be refused."

"Well, the Megadapt people seem to want only one student."

A tense feeling pervaded. The mood changed suddenly when Mr. Chips, coming through on his downstairs tour of duty, startled them all.

"Maybe you should set him outside," Mrs. Powell suggested. "To see how the grass is growing."

As Kevin moved the robot out the side door, he noticed

two black cars parked in the driveway across the road. More Megadapt people, he assumed.

Mr. Chips had his Exterior pattern in action only a short while before Kevin noticed an indicator glowing. The receiver light on its side panel was blinking. Another incoming message awaited him on his PIRX printer.

Fortunately, his mother and sister had left the area near the computer system. The youth quietly tore off the short page. It was a follow-up report from Lindy Woods.

Back in his room, Kevin puzzled over this latest data. Now that his best friend was being interviewed by people from Megadapt Research, who could he turn to for advice?

Pamela. The answer was obvious. Kevin knew his sister would keep the secret. She also had an intuitive talent for problem-solving.

"If Satellite News is investigating, you'll have to cooperate," she said later. "But demand your privacy. Your name has to stay out of it."

"But what if I get called as a witness?"

"Trust her judgment. A good journalist protects her sources, even in a court of law."

Kevin had to agree with his sister. Sometimes, the clarity of her thinking, and her succinct way of summarizing things, surprised him. There was no denying her argument. Lindy Woods and the Satellite News Network team knew an important story and were pursuing it!

"Okay," he finally said. "I'll work out a reply and send it over the modem scrambler."

Kevin showed the first version of his letter to Pamela. She made several suggestions, which he incorporated. Then he sat down at the computer keyboard in his room to prepare the final text. His word processor scanned the message for grammar and spelling.

He addressed the transmission codes using the scrambler tone that Lindy Woods had specified. Then Kevin lifted the telephone handle, and the modem connection switched over. The classified data left his room in beeps and tones, registering at an office in the distant city.

Before getting ready for bed, Kevin pulled the blinds across the window. He saw Mr. Chips still pacing on the entrance walkway.

"Can't leave him out all night," he thought.

Taking care not to disturb his mother or sister, Kevin crept through the hallway toward the door. Outside, he heard a car engine starting up. And Mr. Chips had vanished!

Kevin hurried over to tap on his sister's bedroom window. There was no reaction.

The vehicle was rolling down the street with its lights off. Thinking that the robot may have been stolen, Kevin ran toward the strange car to try to get its license number.

Suddenly, a figure moved from the shadows. Before he could scream or resist, Kevin was grabbed from behind and forced into the rear seat of the car!

CHAPTER 11

Kidnapped K-bits

"He's been kidnapped!"

The Stanton Police Department responded to the distress call within minutes. Sergeant Dalby stood in the front room of the Powell home. While Pamela sat worrying, Mrs. Powell spoke to a man in a dark vehicle parked outside.

"Sorry for the alarm," she said on her return. "I've had everything clarified."

"That's all right, Mrs. Powell," the sergeant smiled. "I thought you would have been notified before it happened."

"That's how the government does things now," she said bitterly.

"They probably didn't want the boy to leave, or come to any harm," the officer said, trying to comfort her. "Good night."

As the policeman left, Mrs. Powell looked sadly at her daughter.

"What did they say?" Pam pleaded. "Was I right?"

"In a way you were, Pam," came the weary response. "Kevin *has* been kidnapped."

"What?!" the girl blurted.

"He's been kidnapped, but not in the usual way. And Thor was with him when it happened."

Pam didn't understand. How could Thor have been there? And why had Sergeant Dalby left?

Pam's confusion was relieved when the Benson family arrived moments later.

Thor recounted to the Powells precisely what had occurred, when they had each played a new laserdisc game in an arcade near the hotel. He described the demonstration at the Alpha-Better exhibit which had left Kevin unconscious. Then, how the crowd had witnessed the boy's voice and brain pattern reproduced at another display.

"This Thought Scanner and MindPrinter," continued Mr. Benson. "The Megadapt people uncovered data that could only have originated with Kevin."

"You mean his brainwaves have been kidnapped?" Pamela asked in wonder.

"Physically he's all right, but something happened to his mind at the convention."

The friction caused by the earlier wrangle over Thor refusing to work for Megadapt was forgotten. The unknown effects of the Thought Scanner were a much more important concern right now.

"What are they going to do with Kevin?" asked Kay. "And why isn't he in a proper hospital?"

Edward Benson led the woman over to a chair. He feared she might collapse from the pressure.

"This is not a normal medical condition," he said in a soft voice. "Mr. Stong and Mr. Norse don't know to what extent his mind has been tapped. Megadapt has the only facility for treating him. As long as Kevin is safe there, we can visit anytime. I suggest tomorrow, mid-morning."

Sleep did not come easily to anyone that night.

In the Megadapt Research A block, a special cot had been prepared for Kevin. He edged onto his bed, watched from behind a two-way mirror. Willard Stong had told him the reason for his being under observation. He explained that they now needed to find out how much of Kevin's stored knowledge had been "borrowed."

Six hours later, the boy was awakened.

"Good morning," said Samuel Norse.

Kevin grumbled a response, clinging to the dream he was having. He was in the workshop lab, helping Thor put the finishing touches on their Tempest-T. The first trial brought in unexpected codes, some kind of military jargon. They added another microcircuit board. Foreign language phrases appeared on the video display monitor. Kevin opened his mouth to speak, but nothing came out. Suddenly, he was attacked by a Doberman pinscher.

"Stop! Get off!"

Sitting bolt upright, Kevin woke with a fright. His cot in the middle of these bare surroundings reminded him where he was.

Samuel Norse entered with a tray containing orange juice and a bowl of cereal. He noticed the boy's cautious, disturbed movements. To relax the youth, he spoke of research projects awaiting him. Kevin was invited to work anywhere in the Experimental Division!

"And yes, your friend Thor will be joining you."

With that to consider, Kevin ate his breakfast.

Two men sat in on a morning session with Kevin and Willard Stong. They had been introduced to Kevin, but the boy had already forgotten their names.

"When you first approached the Alpha-Better booth at the convention, what did you ask the attendants?"

"The first thing?" Kevin flashed back to that encounter. "I asked what the origin of the model was."

This response satisfied Stong. He had asked a control question, used to base the response levels for other answers. For the next two hours, Kevin went over each detail of his experience: how he fell unconscious under the Thought Scanner; his reaction to seeing a 3-D hologram of his brain replayed; how Dr. Fuentes impressed him; the familiar-looking translator; and what occurred during the final seconds before the disturbance broke out.

"And the arcade game?"

Kevin did not know what Stong meant.

"Earlier in the day, prior to entering the hotel," Willard patiently recounted, "you played an interactive laserdisc game called *'Biofeedback Fractions'*."

"I did?"

The three men whispered in hushed tones to each other. For some reason, the episode was blocked out of the boy's mind.

The two men implored Willard to try the surprise link.

"*Biofeedback Fractions* is owned by Alpha-Better."

Kevin Powell, a very receptive subject, yawned.

"What we need to know is whether the Tempest-T plans were removed from your mind," said Willard Stong.

His two associates leaned forward earnestly.

"I'm real tired," Kevin mumbled, after a long pause. "Can't think of anything now."

The men had a short conference.

"Fine," said Willard. "We'll resume this afternoon."

Kay Powell watched her son sleeping.

"He looks peaceful," she remarked, observing him on a video screen.

The office wall behind Willard Stong had a series of monitors recording the boy's cardiovascular signs, brain wavelengths and other functions.

"He's resting more soundly," Stong told the concerned mother. "Undoubtedly, the commotion upset him."

"How long will he have to stay here?"

"Until we know exactly what has occurred. And by that I mean, just what was taken from him. The only positive way is for him to assist in our laboratory."

"Will that be a problem?"

"Not with his friend here. We spoke to the Bensons, and they have given permission for Thor to assist," Willard said, adjusting his CompuBlindsight spectacles. "It has been our intention at Megadapt to attract the brightest young minds from around the country. I'm sorry it couldn't have happened under more relaxing circumstances."

"I appreciate that," Kay Powell replied. "But what about the aftereffects? How will he behave when this is resolved?"

"You know him better than I do, of course. I won't mislead you, but we are sailing in unchartered waters."

Mrs. Powell straightened in her seat.

"We have a crew transferring the contents of Thor Benson's lab here. It may give Kevin the reassurance and comfort he needs."

Thor Benson accompanied the moving truck to the Megadapt Research Facility. He pointed out where each piece of equipment was to be set. Within three hours, a vacant storage hangar had been converted into a functioning lab.

"Mr. Norse," Thor spoke into the intercom.

Seconds later, Samuel Norse appeared on the screen for a two-way conversation.

"Everything delivered properly?"

"Perfect. Just wanted to know, what happens to this new Tempest-T after we build it?" Thor smiled over at Kevin, who had just been escorted out to the lab.

"You keep it, of course."

"For the Stanton Science Fair?" prodded Thor.

"With our best wishes."

They exchanged goodbyes, as the screen went blank.

"That's just the inspiration we need," Thor said to his friend and science partner. "Take that drawer out, pull up the Visucoder, then fire on the ultra-blueprints!"

"Right!" Kevin whispered. "Just like old times."

On the security monitors behind his desk, Willard Stong saw the boys launch into their assignment. Samuel Norse nodded his approval. The men from Megadapt were recording every step in the procedure to develop a new invention.

CHAPTER 12

Phase Jitters

Over the next thirty-six hours, Thor Benson and Kevin Powell assembled the Tempest-T Model II. They took periodic comfort breaks when necessary. Delicious food platters arrived without fanfare. Requests for components and tools were filled promptly. A job had to be done, and the boys willingly complied.

The strain began to show on Kevin during the micro-clustering stage. A visorlike gadget on his head increased the visible scale of the light spectrum. By concentrating on the obscured portions of the spectrum, and using a reference wavelength from a laser pulse, infinite arrangements became possible. Miniscule fractions apart on this invisible light spectrum meant the difference between success and failure.

"Going to take a break?"

Thor seemed puzzled as his friend began to step back from the fluorescent bench. Kevin wavered slightly, then slumped into a chair.

"Not a bad idea, Thor. I need to brighten up before the hard part begins."

"Yeah, we've been going at it real steady. There's no rush."

"There sure is," countered Kevin. "The sooner we show them this can be done, the faster we'll be out of here."

At this last statement, Thor pointed up to the ceiling. Inside one of the outlets which normally held an emergency water sprinkler, was a video camera!

"Well, knock my socks off," whistled Kevin. "How did you catch sight of that?"

Thor had him bend over the electronscope, while a xerold concave lens rotated underneath. The movement of a zooming video camera was reflected clearly.

"If they wanted pictures, I could have asked Pam to drop by," chuckled Kevin.

"Maybe we'll get a copy of the tape from them. Use it for the Science Fair display," suggested Thor. "We have to remember those fancy setups from the convention. Getting the people to the booth is half the battle."

Willard Stong was listening intently.

"Are you pleased with their progress?" Samuel Norse asked him, as they watched the bank of monitors.

"So far. First-class audio and video surveillance. There isn't a microdesign he's added that we won't be able to mass produce," reported Stong. "Too bad we can't make them stay and develop other instruments."

"Well, you know the problems."

"Is there a chance?"

"Unfortunately not," stated Norse.

Willard Stong sighed. "Pity."

For the boys working in the cavernous, electronic-laden laboratory, their main thoughts were of fresh air and completion. The critical part of the Tempest-T assembly was now in progress.

"Stamper One."

The microcircuitry was soldered in a blaze from the laser beam.

"Stamper Two . . . Three . . . Four . . . Five . . . "

Each time Kevin called out, Thor opened the control lens, which pulsed the laser beam through the design pattern.

"And that should do it," came a relieved whisper.

The boys seemed satisfied that the imprinting was successful.

"Before we turn this over, I want to modify its transactivator," whispered Thor, so quietly that the microphone would not detect his words.

Using the electronscope and xerold concave lens to disguise his actions from the overhead camera, Thor slipped in a fibre-optic thread. It traced a near-invisible loop around the transmitter.

"That does it," he breathed.

The youths stepped back from the newly recreated device. Traditional handshakes were exchanged.

The Tempest-T Model II was completed.

An escort guard appeared at the entrance.

"Would you follow us, please?"

The boys fell into step, anticipating congratulations. As the guards walked in front and behind them, Thor and Kevin exchanged concerned looks; this was not the direction to Willard Stong's office. A Doberman pinscher prowled across the hallway.

A sign identified this area as being for "Medical Personnel Only." Their escort pressed a button on the wall. A sliding door came apart, as a man in surgeon's clothing walked by. Kevin and Thor stepped through, as the door slid silently closed behind them.

Samuel Norse greeted them.

"Working very hard, I hear. Satisfied with the new model completed?"

"I will be, once we get a chance to test it," Kevin told him. "But what we really need is a walk outside. Too much air conditioning."

"That will have to wait, Kevin," replied Samuel Norse. "We still have another examination for you. But as far as Thor is concerned, he's free to go."

Thor looked over to his friend and wondered what to do. Leaving Kevin here did not seem fair. But if further medical tests were required, then it was proper he should leave.

"Okay?" he wondered.

Kevin laughed. "Go on, Thor, get a head start."

As Thor was escorted from the area, Kevin raised his voice and shouted, "Leave a few lungfulls for me!"

A number of details remained to be settled before Thor could be released. He was taken into the Administration block, to the office of Willard Stong.

"We're planning further research in this area," Stong told Thor. "We'd appreciate your reviewing these transcripts."

The computer-assisted blind man excused himself and left the room. Thor was left with one escort and a lengthy procedure. He marvelled at how quickly Megadapt had reproduced their exact words and a description of their lab activity. Data and graphics poured out of the desktop display monitor. Thor quickly realized that their assembly methods for the Tempest-T could be duplicated by anyone who had access to this data program!

"Fine," replied his impassive escort, when Thor gave final approval. "I'll have Mr. Stong issue your clearance."

At least an hour had passed since he left Kevin. Thor

wondered what his friend was experiencing. The escort guard had not yet returned. Idly, Thor turned Stong's desktop computer around and typed in "CODE REQUEST."

"ENTER YOUR NAME AND OFFICE," responded the notice on the display monitor.

What should he do? Using the only name and office number he knew for certain, Thor typed in his response.

"WILLARD STONG. D701."

"THANK YOU, D701, MR. STONG," the monitor read. Then names of Megadapt staff, sections, experiments, and outside personnel lit up the screen. "WHICH DO YOU REQUEST?"

"CODE: DATA ENCRYPTION STANDARD KEY," Thor typed.

The computer hesitated.

Thor heard footsteps in the hallway. The thumping of his heart almost drowned them out, as Thor whistled nervously under his breath.

"C*94Dk39*Ee^2*G + 3 – R**"

Thor stared at the screen. He must memorize the complicated sequence! He read it forwards and backwards, trying to think up a word series to help him remember it. Suddenly, the screen went blank.

"HAVE A NICE DAY, MR. STONG," the computer signed off.

Willard Stong entered the room not ten seconds later. He found an animated boy pacing the floor.

"I was away longer than I expected," he explained.

"I don't mind," Thor said, trying to suppress his glee.

"The program and graphics are in order?"

The boy nodded.

Willard Stong adjusted his CompuBlindsight system under the ultraviolet lighting rack in the hallway. He led the boy through the maze toward the main lobby.

A group of people were gathered in one corner. By their clothing, shoulder bags, and cameras, Thor identified them as tourists.

"I thought this facility was off-limits."

"It is," Stong reiterated. "Occasionally though, we will host foreign dignitaries and scientists."

A security guard approached when Stong beckoned.

"See that this lad is brought home safely," he told the guard. Then, turning to Thor, he said, "Thank you again for your assistance."

"What about Kevin?"

"Oh?" The man did not seem very concerned. "He will be released when the proper tests are concluded. His mother knows and has given permission."

They shook hands. Stong strode over to the group of foreigners. Several recognized him and milled about. Samuel Norse was speaking with others on the far side.

"We have a car waiting," the guard said, in a flat tone.

At the front security gatehouse, traffic was halted entering and leaving. Thor sat patiently in the back seat, waiting for the barrier pole to be raised. On the far side of the entrance was a vehicle identical to his.

Its uniformed chauffeur handed some papers to a duty guard. He looks familiar, Thor thought. In a flash of recognition, he identified the man as the translator from the convention.

Looking into the car, Thor saw the chauffeur's single passenger. The mysterious Dr. Fuentes was coming into the Megadapt Research Facility!

CHAPTER 13
Mind Games

At home, Thor Benson tried desperately to reach his father on the family's RND microcomputer. The direct-link code to his new work station at Megadapt did not respond. Edward's personal electronic paging device had been lost at the convention. Even the staff at his midtown office could not contact him.

"I'm on my own with this," Thor said to himself.

He thought he might get a break by plugging into the Facility's Data Encryption Standard Key. Since all of his equipment was still sitting in that Megadapt room—very sly of them, he realized—Thor would have to rely on Kevin's gear. In fact, most of it had originally been Thor's. He'd passed it on to his neighbour when his had been updated.

Thor deactivated the surveillance alarm on Mr. Chips and set the robot against the Powells' side door. Its electromagnet shifted the lock to open. Thor hurried to Kevin's workroom.

The Multiplex Cruncher had broken countless codes. Originally Mr. Benson's research model, Thor had advanced its switcher to bypass the binary system of most older computers. Edward was delighted that his son had been able to develop a systems cruncher from such an outmoded machine.

There was only a remote possibility that he would hit on the right combination of numbers, signs and letters from the start. So much had been happening, and his nerves and mind were strained from a lack of sleep. But Thor began typing different mixes onto the Multiplex Cruncher, in the hope that he'd hit on the code he'd seen in Stong's office.

Again and again the Cruncher's output read "NEGATIVE."

A long period of contemplation followed. With a final bit of instinctive daring, he entered three more versions of the hazy Data Encryption Standard Key code and pressed another sequence of buttons to let the Cruncher spin through the billions of possibilities.

"All I can do is my best," were his thoughts, as he drifted off to sleep.

The Multiplex Cruncher hummed persistently.

A distinguished group had gathered in a comfortable lounge at the Megadapt Research Facility. Drinks and hors d'oeuvres were available. A celebration was in progress. The sounds of numerous foreign languages filled the air. Gradually, a hush came over the room as a side curtain opened, and Willard Stong appeared.

"Welcome to Megadapt, home of tomorrow's innovations." He touched his CompuBlindsight system as he said, "If anyone is aware of the great strides technology can achieve, it is myself. If we can make the blind see, then the world is ours. And this day, gentlemen, we can introduce a device to revolutionize human communications."

This was the same group of dignitaries Thor had seen

earlier in the main lobby and they shifted closer to the front as Stong continued.

"This corporation's founder, Mr. John Dunn, is on a year's leave of absence. In this time, Samuel Norse and myself have established a super-sensitive program unknown to anyone, even our founder."

Stong paused for emphasis. "Megadapt has been experimenting with that most unique and mysterious of all computers—the human brain!"

Some scientists were listening to a simultaneous translation on portable receivers, and the effect of many voices repeating the same speech in different languages was stirring.

"And through one of our secret subsiduary companies, Alpha-Better, we have conducted a special test marketing of the Thought Scanner. It is capable of reading and recording the very waves traveling across the brain synapses where thoughts occur. But what to do with it?" Willard Stong asked.

At the snap of his fingers, an assistant wheeled over a wide cart. On it was the Thought Scanner, resembling a modified medical probe computer terminal. Beside it rested the MindPrinter, a spherical glass object with an assembly of parallel microchip circuits mounted inside. The assistant flicked on a ruby laser pulse, and the components began to interact.

Suddenly, a 3-D hologram of the human brain appeared in midair. Electrical impulses raced along it, tracing thought patterns. Enclosed in a glowing white head without recognizable features, it had a ghostly presence.

The voice of the projection was heard: "What is the origin of this model?. . . Can you really trace the electrical flow through the synapses?. . . I doubt that!"

The scientists laughed. To see a three-dimensional hologram ask itself if it was indeed real, seemed hilarious. No one who was laughing was aware that these words came from a young boy now undergoing an alarming examination nearby.

While the group was still amazed by this part of the demonstration, Willard Stong called their attention to the back of the room. Samuel Norse was entering, followed by two Megadapt guards, who were bringing a stainless steel wagon through the passage.

"Now to introduce Megadapt's crowning achievement, the Tempest-T!"

The scientists swarmed forward to surround the new arrival. Each man closely surveyed the intricate board, admired the crossed peripheral enclosure, the sleek patterning, and the crafted microassembly.

A meek-looking gentleman, bearing a strong resemblance to the great physicist Niels Bohr, leaned over to Norse.

"And what, exactly, does it do?" he asked.

Samuel Norse gladly related his version of the Tempest-T's development.

"You are familiar with the issue of Computer Storms?"

Most nodded in understanding.

"We wanted to find a device that would pick up signals or wavelengths escaping from our mainframe computers. As you know, every movement sets off a discharge of particles into the atmosphere. Each tone, switch, light flash, and tape frequency, results in a measurable degree of positive or negative charges. Most we can decipher, but distance has been a problem. How can one separate specific waves from the countless other electron emissions swirling in the air?"

A few scientists shook their heads.

"Here is the answer," Norse stated, touching the device. "Tempest for 'storm', T for 'transactor'."

Side by side were the Thought Scanner, the MindPrinter and the Tempest-T.

"When I informed you, gentlemen, of our invention to revolutionize human communication, it was not an exaggeration," declared Willard Stong. "This Tempest-T, when coupled to our Alpha-Better pair, is capable of pulling in the actual brainwaves from any person, located anywhere this laser beam reaches!"

As Stong paused to allow his words to sink in, a few exclamations of disbelief could be heard around the room.

"We may tune in to an individual's brainwave frequency over any distance with Tempest-T, record every electrical impulse using our Thought Scanner, and finally, duplicate the results on this MindPrinter!"

The astounding possibilities swept over the audience, everyone seemed to be talking at once.

"Able to read minds at a distance?"

"It will enhance state security!"

"No more interrogations! Just point the beam!"

"We could know what anybody, even the president, is thinking of doing the moment an idea comes into his mind!"

"Science has achieved the ultimate!"

Everyone present shared a secret desire to use this unique surveillance system for his own benefit. But slowly, a realization began to dawn among them. Their own thoughts were probably being recorded!

"Is it operating now?" someone demanded.

"Not at the moment," Stong said.

An audible sigh of relief came back at him.

"Are there any questions?"

No one spoke up. Some people were beginning to feel intimidated.

"Then perhaps we will demonstrate how this unified system works in public," Willard said. "Our single input requirement is an individual's brainwave pattern. Just like fingerprints, each person's is different."

"Then how do you manage to key into someone else's mind?" asked one of the scientists, through an interpreter. "In effect, how can you fingerprint someone without his knowing it?"

"Simple. We make it a game."

"*Biofeedback Fractions* is an interactive laserdisc video arcade game from our private subsidiary, Alpha-Better," Samuel Norse explained. "This game is a test market unit for us to acquire a large databank. In it, the player dons a helmet that identifies his alpha-waves, registers them in our mainframe computer, then makes a game of letting the player synchronize with his beta-waves."

"By replaying our tapes of these sessions, which people unknowingly pay us to take, we can find out who they are, what their occupation is, and anything else we may consider valuable for future reference." Stong paused for a moment. "And now, we are preparing a home version of *Biofeedback Fractions*!"

"So you realize, gentlemen," Norse concluded, "Everyone who participates becomes a slave to our master machine!"

Time seemed to stop, as a deathly silence settled over the room.

In another room of the Megadapt Research Facility, a

boy of sixteen felt his mind leave his body. Just for a moment.

"Where am I?"

"Where would you like to be?" asked an old voice.

"Home."

"Then that is where you are," it suggested.

The boy stirred. A smile came onto his face. He remained unconscious.

"Thank you."

Under the piercing light of a medical probe, the boy's eyelids were lifted open. For an instant, the reflection in the dark pupil showed a person bending over him.

Somewhere in his thoughts, Kevin Powell saw the image of Dr. Fuentes, extremely close to him.

CHAPTER 14

An Involved Reporter

"Leave this property at once."

The strange inhuman voice came from the bushes by the Powell's house and was addressed to a woman in tennis attire making her way across the front lawn.

"Warning. Identify yourself."

The woman raised her sunglasses to observe the approaching robot.

"Identify yourself," Mr. Chips repeated. "Or leave the property at once!"

Down the street in a parked van, two Megadapt Research observers watched the woman through their OptoScopes. They wondered how this gorgeous neighbor had escaped previous notice. Because of the residents, 207 and 208 Matrix Boulevard were being closely watched.

Alerted by an internal monitor, Pamela Powell came to the front door.

"Are you lost?" she asked.

"Kevin Powell's home?" the woman inquired.

"Yes," Pam said. Then she recognized the visitor and opened the door to her. "Welcome to Stanton!"

Pamela checked to ensure that the Megadapt van

remained parked down the street. Then she led the woman through to her brother's workroom.

"That's some disguise," Pam told her. "You fit right into this neighborhood."

"Just how I wanted it," came the reply.

Pamela tapped gently on the closed workroom door.

"What is it now?" Thor's tone indicated irritation.

Pam opened the door, and the visitor entered.

"Lindy Woods!"

Thor sat back in his chair, startled by the surprise arrival of the Satellite News reporter.

"I drove from the city to avoid detection on any flight lists. My crew is parked two streets away," she explained. "Hopefully, your house-watchers were fooled by my tennis clothes."

"That van and two others have been here awhile," Thor told her. "We still don't know what's going on at Megadapt."

Lindy Woods flashed her famous smile, as she lifted a slim box out of the sports bag on her shoulder.

"Floppies. Everything you ever wanted to know about Megadapt Research, but were afraid to ask."

Thor began to load the floppy disks into a Q-Drive. This gave protection from computer storm tracers similar to the Tempest-T. The Q-Drive had a lead and platinum shield that stopped electron emissions, so that the data displayed would remain confined to this room.

"I'm grateful you returned Kevin's message," he told the reporter. "I thought Pam was playing a trick on me."

"I'd never do that," chuckled the girl.

"The message was perfectly timed. One of our field reporters was investigating the Alpha-Better Teaching Method Plan for schools," she continued. "And then I filmed that segment on the *Biofeedback Fractions* game.

Did that ever get a response! It's now the video arcade mystery. For some reason, people playing it are reporting delayed hallucinations, as if their minds are being lifted from them."

"And what did the field reporter conclude?"

Lindy paused before answering.

"Nothing. He was murdered yesterday."

For the first time since the bizarre set of circumstances had begun with the arrival of Willard Stong, a terrifying dread gripped Thor and Pamela. If the Megadapt conspiracy had murdered a reporter, what would it do to them?

Meanwhile, the data was being released onto the display terminal. The Megadapt Report had a frightening scope. Since Samuel Norse and Willard Stong had assumed control from the absent founder, Megadapt had behaved like a private country. People whom the federal government had classified as dangerous, Megadapt granted research funds. To leaders in foreign dictatorships, Megadapt supplied high-tech military data. It seemed that whatever was good for Megadapt was bad for the nation.

"Why hasn't something been done?" Thor demanded.

"Sometimes a disaster has to occur before action is taken," Lindy Woods admitted. "Take a look at these other companies. Recognize any?"

A list of fourteen computer-related companies popped onto the screen. Several were located in Stanton.

"Sure do," Thor replied. "Kids at school are working there during job semesters."

Lindy turned, to say in a grave tone, "Each one is a secret subsidiary of Megadapt. Just like Alpha-Better."

Three bells struck. The Multiplex Cruncher was sounding.

"What now?" the reporter asked.

Thor shifted the cardboard carton blocking the Cruncher. He peered into the small viewing section at its core bracket.

"This is matching a code that I saw at Megadapt. I forgot the exact sequence, but not the actual symbols. The Multiplexer has been working all night trying to match them to a Data Encryption Standard Key code. And we might have it!"

"C*94Dk39*Ee^2*G + 3 – R**"

"Fantastic!" shouted Pam.

"I'll try it out," Thor declared.

"No you won't!" Lindy challenged.

"What? This is the entry code to their most private files!" Thor blurted. "We've got them!"

"And what will you do?"

"Call the police. And have Kevin released!"

"Think it over," Lindy Woods said softly. "You are an external computer calling up their mainframe, right? Whatever answer comes back will be addressed directly to this house."

"And two minutes later, those men in the van will be knocking at our door," Pam added. "With sledgehammers."

"Any suggestions?" Thor asked.

"Give me the D.E.S. code, and I'll hand it to the top person in the country."

Thor knew her position as head of the President's Council for Physical Fitness. Her expression left no doubt that Lindy Woods had direct access to the Oval Office.

A plan was set. Although Thor did not have a driver's license, he knew how to handle a car. He was the first to leave the house. As he drove Kevin's sports car out of the driveway, the Megadapt van started up and followed at a distance.

Pamela called up two girlfriends and met them, moments later, on the front lawn. The remaining Megadapt observer pulled up to chat with the trio.

This provided an escape cover for Lindy Woods. Wearing one of Mrs. Powell's housecoats and holding a cup, she walked casually across the lawn, as if on her way to a neighborhood coffee klatch. Two streets away, the reporter climbed into the small truck where her crew was waiting. It sped off toward the Cartesian Freeway.

"Kevin. Can you hear me?"

The voice faded in and out of the boy's mind.

Edward Benson leaned over the extended lounge chair to look closely at the boy. As he began to speak again, he was silenced by the arrival of Dr. Fuentes and the translator. They nodded to Mr. Benson.

"His brilliance has brought him to exhaustion," relayed the interpreter. "We suggest he remain under our observation for another forty-eight hours."

"I disagree. What Kevin needs most is a change of surroundings," Edward told them. "His mother can take better care of him."

"We detect animosity. Are you unhappy over your contract?"

Edward Benson withheld the ferocity of his opinions. As a professional consultant, he knew that, sometimes, the wisest thing to say was nothing at all.

"If that is your wish, we will arrange his departure."

The two men left, and Edward was relieved. He raised the boy's arm.

"You're going home, Kevin. Do you hear me?"

Kevin blinked his eyes slowly and smiled.

"I'm really beat. How long have I slept?"

"Too long."

"My head feels like a milkshake."

Assisted to his feet, Kevin looked around the room. He suddenly recalled nightmares from another Megadapt area. He was incapable of realizing this was the result of an all-night session under the Thought Scanner.

"Mr. Benson, sorry to see that you're leaving us," Samuel Norse said, when they arrived at the main lobby.

"Just taking the boy home," replied Edward. "I'll be back later."

"No, you won't. We have terminated your contract. Severance pay will be transferred to your personal account. Goodbye."

His dismissal was a comfort. Over the last two days, Edward Benson had become convinced that Megadapt's affairs were not legitimate. Unfortunately, he had failed to break into certain data files and hadn't been able to confirm his suspicions.

Kevin remained passive and quiet during the drive home. An obvious reaction to the fatigue and strain, thought Edward.

Laraine Benson phoned Stanton High School and spoke to Kay Powell, explaining that Kevin had arrived home. Not to alarm the woman, she did not comment on the boy's condition.

"I'm leaving now," Mrs. Powell told her.

Pamela prepared Kevin's bed, as Mr. Benson helped the unsteady youth to his room. Kevin fell asleep as soon as he lay down.

"The news is out," Pamela whispered.

"What do you mean?" asked Edward Benson.

"Anytime now, the truth about Megadapt will be released!"

He wanted to hear the whole story, but he had another concern first. "Where's Thor?"

Pamela shrugged, not daring to answer.

CHAPTER 15

Reverse the Charges

The sports car weaved through traffic along Interface Avenue. Each time Thor checked the rear view mirror, he saw the same van behind him. Being a decoy for Lindy Woods's escape had seemed like a good idea at the time, but now Thor wondered how long these Megadapt Research observers intended to track him.

One thing was certain. The Satellite News Network report would be broadcast in ninety minutes. And Thor knew exactly what the contents of their Exclusive Bulletin would be.

The signs of fast food outlets along the way reminded the boy of the two meals he was missing. Thor turned left onto Grafex Street. This was the shortest route to the Big Byte. If the men trailing him did not want to eat there, he chuckled, tough for them.

The Megadapt van parked at the edge of the parking lot, as Thor entered the restaurant. He resisted looking back at the pursuit vehicle, trying to remain calm.

On one television set in the Big Byte, a notice flashed across the bottom of the screen. "SPECIAL PRESIDENTIAL ANNOUNCEMENT UPCOMING." Between bites of his double club sandwich, Thor spoke to the new man behind the counter. He asked him what he thought the president might announce.

"I've got no idea," the attendant replied. "But I'll tell you what I'd do if I was president. Close up all these crazy arcade places!"

"There's nothing wrong with them," Thor said, surprised at the man's vehemence.

"You kiddin'? Not only are those laser video arcades taking money out of the pockets of kids who can't afford it," continued the agitated man, "but now the kids are being sent to hospitals!"

"Fights can happen anywhere," muttered Thor.

"Not fights. I mean freakouts!" The attendant pointed to the Arkade located in the plaza. "We had three ambulances there today! Stupid kids put money into this new game, *Fractions* or something, the next minute they wake up in hospital forgetting who they are!"

Thor nearly choked on his sandwich.

He walked quickly across to the Arkade, but found that the *Biofeedback Fractions* booth was gone. The usual number of kids and young adults were playing other laserdisc games. A few were plugged into *MusikMaker*, composing and conducting instant rock operas. One man was exchanging money for carbon tokens.

"Do you still have the *Fractions* booth?"

"Out of bounds," came the reply. "Manager's orders."

"But did you ship it back?" Thor demanded.

The man eyed him warily. "Naw, it's downstairs. We'll just wait till all the fuss dies down. Come back next week."

Thor did not say that *Biofeedback Fractions* would be required much sooner.

The headlights of the Megadapt van dimmed, as Thor

parked in front of his home. Mr. Chips's shadowy form could be seen, still on its security rounds.

"Kevin's fast asleep," Pam told him.

Thor stood in the Powells' living room and heard the details of Kevin's release.

"I think we should take him to the hospital," Mrs. Powell said, greatly concerned. "He could be in a coma."

Mr. Benson and his wife came across the road to see their son. Thor's father was particularly upset.

"Why were you driving that car!?" he demanded.

"It was an emergency, Dad."

"You don't even have a license!" the man raged.

Thor knew he had bent the rules too far this time.

"And you left the lights on," his mother added.

The matter was dropped for the time, as Edward Benson asked whether there had been any change in Kevin's condition.

Thor brought his father the news that Alpha-Better's Thought Scanner, Mind Printer and *Biofeedback Fractions* game were really part of Megadapt Research.

"And I know they're responsible for Kevin being unconscious now," he stated. "Stong and Norse wanted us lucid long enough to reconstruct another Tempest-T. Then Dr. Fuentes arrived, and I'm positive he did more tests on Kevin than they told us about."

Mr. Benson contemplated the situation. He realized that if Kevin's mental health was to be restored, drastic measures would have to be taken.

"Did you leave a backdoor key in that Tempest-T?"

The others recognized the term used to describe a designer's secret access mode to enter his own invention after it has been shipped out. A "backdoor key" bypasses all later passwords.

"I know you've put one in everything you've helped me on," Edward added.

The boy reacted with a burst of enthusiasm.

"Mrs. Powell, can you get to that room where some of the Science Fair exhibits are stored?" he asked.

The woman shook her head.

"I can't, not at this hour."

Thor turned to Pamela.

"But Mr. Chips can!" he exclaimed. "The alarm shut-off and lock-demagnetizer program is still in his circuit panel. It's waiting to be used for the Fair, but we can put one of those displays to good use now!"

It took a moment for the boy to explain his idea. Once they'd heard his plan, everyone agreed to cooperate.

In the workroom, Thor gathered together a special telephone modem and a set of microelectronic jumper cables. He was ready for action.

First, the Megadapt observers had to be distracted. Mrs. Powell loaded Mr. Chips into the station wagon for his role in the mission. Laraine Benson started her car, and as each vehicle accelerated away in opposite directions, both Megadapt vehicles followed in pursuit. The ploy had worked.

"Kevin, wake up. Fast!"

Thor shook his friend roughly. He had to get Kevin out of the house quickly. Mr. Benson helped his son lift Kevin into the rear seat of the sports car.

Edward took the wheel, and they raced down the street and onto the entrance ramp of the Cartesian Freeway.

Police sirens screamed past them. Military trucks with armed soldiers in the back followed. Thor noticed a mass of flashing lights as they passed a familiar exit. The police and military were converging on the Megadapt Facility!

Edward Benson increased his speed. Suddenly, an unmarked police car flashed alongside and forced them from the road.

"Dalby! It's about time!" Edward shouted.

The officer came back to their vehicle, saw Kevin's limp form, and responded immediately to Mr. Benson's request for an escort.

"I thought that new company was up to something," the officer told them, as he ran back to his car. "Follow me!"

Pamela pressed the side panel on Mr. Chips's arm. The robot's demagnetizer program took over. It swung across the lock assembly inside the main entrance at Stanton High School. The alarm system was automatically switched off.

"Which room is it?" Pam asked.

"I don't know. We'll just have to check them all," replied her mother.

They dashed into the section of the school where the Science Fair exhibits were kept in storage. The room-by-room search ended with a frantic question.

"Is this it?" Kay Powell gasped.

She held up the display case for the Fibre-Optic Transducer.

"I think so," Pam replied. "It's the closest thing to it."

Pamela carried the display case containing the Transducer and followed her mother back out to the station wagon. They reloaded Mr. Chips and drove off.

Sergeant Dalby led the sports car into the plaza parking lot. Alerted by the screeching tires, customers from the Big Byte came out to watch the action.

Kevin had fallen unconscious again. The police officer

and Mr. Benson lifted the boy out. Thor had his own hands filled with electronic gear he'd brought from home.

"Where's the *Fractions* booth?" Thor asked the stunned attendant in the Arkade.

"I told ya, buddy, out of order."

Sergeant Dalby and Edward Benson entered, carrying the insensible boy.

"Police emergency!" Dalby barked.

"Okay, but you'll have to answer to the owner," muttered the attendant.

He led them through a milling throng of games players to the back stairs. In the basement, where broken machines were stored, the *Biofeedback Fractions* booth occupied a center space.

A commotion erupted on the stairway. Mrs. Powell and Pamela forced their way through and downstairs.

"I hope this is it," Pamela said.

Thor took the Fibre-Optic Transducer from her.

"You did great, Pam."

He set the display case on the floor and opened his bag of electronic equipment.

"I need a telephone," Thor shouted.

By this point, the dismayed night attendant was prepared to help in any way. He brought the telephone extension from upstairs and plugged it into a nearby socket. Meanwhile, Mr. Benson settled Kevin inside the laserdisc game booth.

The Fibre-Optic Transducer display case was cracked open. Its main component featured a fibre-optic thread loop, stretched over a dilating silicon disk. Just as Thor began to attach wires between the Transducer and the telephone, he banged his fist in despair.

"What's wrong?" asked his father.

"Blast!" Thor cursed. "Megadapt still has my laser pulser! This Transducer needs that laser for a transfer."

The Arkade attendant pointed to a machine in the corner. It was a recent *Ace of Space* laserdisc game.

"How about that?" he shouted. "Only thing broken is its token collector."

"Maybe," said Thor hopefully.

Using their combined expertise, Thor and his father extracted the laser unit from the arcade game. Since this laser was used solely for reading images off the rotating game disk, it was a perfect substitute for his own pulser.

They assembled a refracting lens housing and directed the laser beam. The test was positive.

Thor reached for his portable modem and attached it to the Arkade telephone. Using the modem's internal microcomputer, he addressed the secret code for Megadapt.

"C*94Dk39*Ee^{2}*G + 3 – R**"

The Data Encryption Standard Key code registered onto the micro's small display panel.

Mr. Benson stood alongside the *Biofeedback Fractions* booth, holding the helmet securely over Kevin's head.

The close basement air was filled with tension.

"YES, MR. STONG." Megadapt's computer was on-line!

"REQUEST ENTRY TO TEMPEST-T," Thor typed.

Moments later, it responded. "ENTRY GRANTED."

With a nod, Thor directed his father to switch the converted arcade laser onto full beam. It blazed through the Transducer at the speed of light. The fibre-optic strand glowed. A connecting wire between the Transducer and the telephone modem jerked. The energy conversion flowed in a transfer between systems.

Suddenly, Kevin's unconscious body shifted. His head, in the enclosed helmet, became agitated.

"Reverse the charges!" Thor screamed.

Samuel Norse and Willard Stong reacted quickly to the invasion of the Megadapt Facility.

The two scientists met in Stong's office. On the overhead security monitors, they witnessed the arrival of the police and government troops.

"Quickly! Alter the code!" Stong shouted.

The Thought Scanner, MindPrinter, and Tempest-T on the desk were linked to Megadapt's mainframe computer. As Norse reached for his encryption card, the Tempest-T began to pulse. Suddenly, the two attached megamachines reacted in unison.

"I can't break in! All three are crashing! Reverse charges!"

In desperation, Willard Stong lurched at the mainframe cables. Sparks flew. His CompuBlindsight visors smashed to the floor. Stong lay groping beside them, his hands burned from the shock.

The glow increased to a white flame. The fibre-optic conversion inside the Tempest-T sent the Thought Scanner and MindPrinter to destruction in a total meltdown!

CHAPTER 16
A Fair Ending

The Stanton Science Fair took place as scheduled, one week later. Local high schools, junior colleges, and technical institutes participated. Many researchers, employed by computer firms, entered their own independent displays. Other personnel toured the event on the lookout for inventions to be licenced.

A mobile crew from the Satellite News Network roved the area. Attention fell on each display booth coming under their lights. The brightest lights followed the charismatic reporter, Lindy Woods.

". . . . and this is another example of Agricultural Science at its source," she was saying, pointing to a scale model of a farm. "Would you like to demonstrate your Time-Delayed Soil Protein Releaser?"

Two students in the exhibit pressed a button, setting the unit into action. Above the tiny fields, a white sun rose and set rapidly. This speeded-up activity gave the illusion of many days of sunshine. A cross-sectional cutout of the field showed four layers of soil becoming more brittle. When a grounded meter reached a specific level, liquid soil protein automatically released itself into the third layer. By seeping upwards, more of the earth's natural nutrients quenched the dry farmland. As a result, farmers could expect more abundant harvests.

Lindy Woods thanked the pair for their explanation of the display. She also congratulated them on the fine contribution they were making for the benefit of everyone.

The camera lights dimmed. As Lindy stepped aside, a young girl waved from the edge of the throng. The reporter caught sight of her.

"Pamela, I wondered where you were," Lindy said. "Nice to have you back in our town. At least this time you don't have to worry about being chased away. Are you going to stop by our exhibit?"

"I'm on my way there now. After all, this is a follow-up to last week's big story—'MicroKidz Crack Megadapt'."

They shared a laugh, feeling good that everything had been justly resolved. Willard Stong and Samuel Norse had been jailed on numerous charges and were not expected to be free for many years. Dr. Fuentes was deported to his homeland, where he was wanted for other crimes. The founder of Megadapt Research, Mr. John Dunn, had cut short his sabbatical and returned to Stanton, in an attempt to save his beleaguered company. The *Biofeedback Fractions* laserdisc games were ordered destroyed. Those players who reported aftereffects were receiving treatment, and full recovery was expected. Kevin Powell, whose keen mind was jolted back to stability in the meltdown of the Megadapt equipment, was in top form.

"And what about your boyfriend?" asked Lindy.

Pamela blushed.

"Please, don't say that while he's listening."

"Oh, he's not really your boyfriend?" Lindy wondered.

"Well, kind of," Pam whispered. "But he doesn't want to admit it."

"Okay, I just want to know how Thor is."

"Back to S.O.P.," the girl smiled. "Standard Operating Procedure."

In a far aisle, Thor Benson wandered the Science Fair, absorbing the latest innovations. He visited the three older students who had developed the Fibre-Optic Transducer. He thanked them for its timing, and they thanked him for its field testing. Thor approached other youngsters whose exhibits he admired.

"Decommissioning?"

The sign hung over a small model of a nuclear reactor. Three junior college girls recognized the boy standing in front of their booth. Each described the procedure to him in very precise terms.

"It has to do with safely disposing of the contents of nuclear reactors once they become obsolete," said the tall girl.

"You see, all nuclear power stations have a certain life expectancy. Once they reach that and exhaust themselves, they become dangerous," added her friend.

The third girl remained silent, nervous about speaking to Stanton's local hero.

Thor would later wish that she had spoken up. For, little did he know that her information would be of vital importance in solving the nuclear reactor mystery in the next MicroKidz adventure, *FISSION CHIPS*.

As Kevin Powell demonstrated the Tempest-T to yet another group, he explained some limitations of the device.

"Our model II was lost in the meltdown, which you may have heard about," he began.

Most people were very aware of the events of the past week. That made the MicroKidz's exhibit the most popular booth of the Fair.

"This is the first model built," he continued. "It was tampered with, but we've done our best to restore it to the original specifications."

He flicked on the power switch. Instantly, a video display monitor lit up, showing the electron data emissions from other computers in the hall. By tuning through the wavelengths, Kevin managed to dial up information from any direction he chose. It was a remarkable display. The Tempest-T deciphered all signals from computer storms into clear programs.

Lindy Woods bumped into Thor Benson near their booth. Pamela had steered her toward the boy.

"There you are!" Lindy approached and kissed him on the cheek. Thor blushed.

"I hope your girlfriend isn't jealous," the reporter joked.

"Pam, what have you been telling her?" he asked.

"Not a thing!" she declared.

"Keep it that way," he smiled at her.

Lindy Woods took Thor by the arm while she spoke.

"So many people are thankful that we managed to remove those bad elements from Megadapt," she confirmed. "I know the president will want to congratulate you personally."

"I just did what was right," he murmured.

"And you also helped bring the victims of that laser-disc game back to full health."

"It only meant reversing the flow through the Tempest-T one more time," he replied, with sincere modesty.

The Satellite News Network crew shifted in front of the trio as the lights came on. Lindy Woods prepared to go on the air, live, with a group interview. The camera signal went on.

"As many of our viewers have requested, we are here in Stanton where the annual Science Fair is being held. However, it is not just the demonstrations or exhibits that are attracting so many people this year. Instead, it is the participation of three youngsters."

She stepped back to the booth where the trio waited nervously.

"Well, ladies and gentlemen, on behalf of all of you, it's time I did something I've always wanted to do." Turning to Pamela, Kevin, and Thor, she handed them her reporter's notebook and asked, "Could I please have your autographs?"

Applause broke out from the surrounding crowd. Kevin signed first, as Thor put his arm around Pamela and waved to the camera.